Organize Simplify Thrive

Clearing Your Way to a Desired Lifestyle

CONSULTANT | EDUCATOR | COACH

SYLVIA Holloway ™

AUTHOR | ADVOCATE | SPEAKER

PUBLISHED BY:

Love to Organize You

1448 E. 52nd Street

Chicago, Illinois 60615

DISCLAIMER AND/OR LEGAL NOTICES

While all attempts have been made to verify information provided in this book and its ancillary materials, neither the author nor publisher assumes responsibility for errors, inaccuracies, or omissions and is not responsible for any monetary loss in any matter. If advice concerning legal, financial, accounting, or related matters is needed, the services of a qualified professional should be sought. This book or its associated ancillary materials, including verbal and written training, is not intended for use as a source of legal, financial, or accounting advice. You should be aware of the various laws governing business transactions or other business practices in your state. The information contained in this book is strictly for educational purposes. Therefore, if you wish to apply ideas contained in this book, you are taking full responsibility for your actions. There is no guarantee or promise, expressed or implied, that you will earn any money using the strategies, concepts, techniques, exercises, and ideas in the book.

STANDARD EARNINGS AND INCOME DISCLAIMER

With respect to the reliability, accuracy, timeliness, usefulness, adequacy, completeness, and/or suitability of information provided in this book, LOVE TO ORGANIZE YOU, its partners' associates, affiliates, consultants, and/ or presenters make no warranties, guarantees, representations, or claims of any kind. Participants' results will vary depending on many factors. All claims or representations as to income earning are not considered as average earnings. All products and services are for educational and informational purposes only. Check with your accountant, attorney, or professional advisor before acting on this or any information. By continuing with reading this book, you agree that Love to Organize You is not responsible for the success or failure of your personal, business, or financial decisions relating to any information.

Printed in the United States of America | FIRST EDITION

Acknowledgments

I am incredibly grateful to the following individuals who have contributed to the creation of this book and supported me throughout this journey:

To my incredible mother, Bobbie Holloway,

I want to express my deepest gratitude for your unwavering love, support, and understanding throughout the countless hours I've dedicated to writing, researching, and serving others.I am profoundly grateful for the amazing circle of friends you've surrounded yourself with, who have become like family to me. Sharon, Gerri, Jennifer, Beverly, Martha, Pearlie - your wisdom, strength, and unwavering support have left an indelible mark on my life. You've covered me in times of need, yet also exposed me to the beauty and complexities of the world, shaping me into the person I am today.

Ma, your love knows no bounds, and your kindness knows no limits. There is no one else I would rather have by my side, cheering me on every step of the way. You are truly the epitome of a remarkable mother, and I am endlessly grateful for your presence in my life.

My clients, the inspiration behind this book and my guiding light in the world of organization. Your patience, dedication to a sustainable life, and commitment to personal growth have deeply influenced my principles and framework, and for that, I am immensely grateful.

My sister Sibyl, thank you for believing that I can do most things. I say most things because a sibling will get you together. You cheer for me so hard and it does not go unnoticed.

My colleagues, coaches (Tiana and Yolanda), friends and beta readers, who provided invaluable feedback, encouragement, and support along the way.

The experts and professionals whose insights and expertise have enriched the content of this book and provided valuable guidance.

Thank you to my dad, Sylvester Holloway, who gave me this educator and entrepreneurial spirit. You have given me countless hours of practice and you've taught me that I'm not better than anyone and no one is better than me. This has allowed me to move in life with pride and grace.

And finally, to the readers - thank you for embarking on this journey with me. May this book empower you to create a more organized and fulfilling life that allows you to live to your full potential, allowing you to thrive!

Table of Contents

Welcome to *"Organize, Simplify, Thrive: Clearing Your Way to a Desired Lifestyle."* In the hustle and bustle of our modern lives, finding a sense of calm and order can often seem like an elusive dream. This book is your companion on a journey to simplify your surroundings, declutter your mind, and pave the way for a thriving and balanced life.

In the pages that follow, you'll discover a holistic approach to organization that goes beyond mere cleaning or straightening up your space. "Organize, Simplify, Thrive" is more like a guide to intentional living, leading you through the transformative process of simplifying to organize your space where you can and will be able to embrace a life of purpose.

This book is divided into thoughtfully crafted sections, each tailored to address different aspects of the process. From tapping into the impact of clutter and identifying your desires for your physical space and knowing that maintenance is achieveable, "Organize, Simplify, Thrive" provides a comprehensive framework to help you achieve lasting order and clarity to move in a direction that is fulfilling for you.

As you embark on this journey, you'll find prompts, quotes, and other reflections to encourage mindful living. Discover and embrace the power of letting go of the unnecessary, making room for what truly matters to you, and experiencing the freedom that comes with an organized and simplified lifestyle.

Remember that this is not just about cleaning up your house; it's about understanding your particular lifestyle to create space for productivity, creativity, meaningful connections, and happiness. "Organize, Simplify, Thrive" is your invitation to embrace an intentional way of living—one that allows you to thrive in every aspect of your life.

Are you ready to unlock the potential of a clutter-free existence? Open the pages of "Organize, Simplify, Thrive" and let the journey begin. Your organized and thriving life awaits.

Organize

LTOY

Part One

Here's to Knowing

"I have discovered in life that there are ways of getting almost anywhere you want to go, if you really want to go."
-Langston Hughes

CHAPTER 1

Impact of Knowing

Over the years, I have met a lot of people and serviced a lot of clients who have a lot in common. Some of my clients are teachers, principals, therapists, realtors, a variety of entrepreneurs, and I've serviced countless retirees. All of these people were clear on the fact that they wanted order. They wanted their home or business or both to be organized and not in a state of confusion. Some of these clients could be classified as hoarders, and some could be classified with OCD, but what I've learned over the years is that we are all yearning for order because we want to thrive.

Irrespective of age, I've observed a common desire among my clients—they yearn for more fulfillment or satisfaction in their lives. Whether embarking on a new business venture, exploring the world through travel, dedicating time to volunteer efforts, or simply enjoying quality moments with family and friends, they all share a collective aspiration for peace of mind. They all want to thrive. The pursuit is not just about sustaining their passions, but also about creating the space and tranquility needed to pursue their unique desires.

Every single client I work with brings their own unique flair and they all share this burning desire to achieve more. I mean, really think about it – they took that step of reaching out to me, a professional organizer, to elevate their lifestyle. That's pretty profound, isn't it? They're fully aware that there's untapped potential within them, and they're hungry for more. The common thread? They yearn to thrive because they're steadfast in the belief that it's not just a possibility; it's their reality in the making.

Where to begin is a whole other question. At times, the clients I've serviced are spot-on about where they want to start their organizational journey. Other times, it's like navigating through a sea of chaos, and they're just unsure where to dive. That's when I throw in a little encouragement—start in a space that'll light up your face. What will put a smile on your face? Simply think of the area in your home that will make you happy or pleased. But, really, it's about picking the spot that you believe will instantly upgrade you, making you feel like a better version of yourself. Is that your bedroom, living room, or maybe it's your kitchen? So, which room will be your instant mood booster?

Write the room(s) that will be an instant mood booster below. In the space provided, write one room or more than one room and explain why you made this selection.

_____

_____

_____

_____

_____

_____

_____

_____

_____

_____

_____

_____

LOOK AT ME . . .

- What aspects are calling for your attention?

- Is it conquering clutter, or are you looking for systems and/or solutions?

- Perhaps, managing time feels like a challenge.

- Maybe you want guidance to pinpoint just exactly what you want.

Maybe you don't really know what you want. We all have varying lifestyles and needs. My route to the office may be shorter or longer than yours. One person may be on a train and a bus where another may be waiting for a ride share. Those are some examples of how different we are. So, whether you're settling into a new space or preparing for a big move, the support you need is tailored to your unique situation.

Let's figure out together what's on your organizational pathway! Please take a moment to fill out this *Organize, Simplify, Thrive*: Baseline Survey.

Mark all that are relevant.

☐ **Conquering Clutter**: Tackle the chaos and create a space that breathes.

☐ **Organizational Systems**: Explore innovative systems to transform your daily life.

☐ **Clarifying Desires**: Pinpoint what you truly desire for a focused and intentional life.

☐ **New Space Setup**: Whether settling in or preparing to move, you want to make your space feel like home.

☐ **Time Management Mastery**: Gain control over your schedule without the juggling act.

☐ **Clutter Control Coaching**: Personalized coaching to master clutter and maintain order.

☐ **Finding Homes for Your Belongings**: Ensuring every item has its designated place for easy access.

☐ **Schedule Management**: Streamline your schedule for increased productivity and balance.

☐ **Shopping for Organizational Tools**: Guidance on selecting the right tools to get organized..

- ☐ **Organizing After a Loss**: Support and strategies for navigating organization during challenging times.

- ☐ **Planning for a New Venture**: Organizational strategies tailored for new ventures.

- ☐ **How to Sort Items**: Expert guidance on effective item sorting methods.

- ☐ **Creating New Habits**: Cultivate sustainable habits that contribute to an organized lifestyle.

- ☐ **Assessing Your Space**: Evaluate and optimize your living or working space for maximum efficiency.

- ☐ **Organizational Coaching**: Receive personalized coaching to develop effective organizational strategies.

- ☐ **Support with Items to Donate**: Assistance in determining which items to donate for a clutter-free environment.

- ☐ **Space Management**: Optimize your space for functionality, aesthetics, and a harmonious atmosphere.

- ☐ **Where to Donate**: Guidance on places to donate items for a positive impact.

- ☐ **What to Trash**: Assistance in identifying items suitable for disposal.

- ☐ **What to Recycle**: Strategies on environmentally friendly disposal options.

- ☐ **How to Categorize**: Tips on effective categorization for streamlined organization.

SURVEY SAYS: "EXPECTATIONS"

No, at this very moment, you're not on *The Family Feud*, but what you want matters and what you say matters. The baseline survey serves as a role in the change process by providing valuable insights into the current state of your affairs and setting a reference point for your future progress. What you expect is very important in this journey. Your expectations matter because they serve as a guide to shape the outcome in various aspects of your life. That's important on so many levels.

The *Organize, Simplify, Thrive*: Baseline Survey serves to reinforce expectations and do the following:

- **Get you motivated**: Expectations can serve as powerful motivators. When we set expectations for ourselves, we're more likely to push ourselves to reach our full potential and strive for excellence.

- **Set direction**: You now know where to point that arrow. You have a sense of direction and purpose to define your goals and standards, guiding you toward what you want to achieve.

- **Influence behavior**: Our expectations influence our actions. It's a mindset because when we expect positive outcomes, we're more likely to approach tasks with confidence and determination. On the other hand, low expectations can lead to doubt and get in the way of progress.

- **Impact relationships**: Yes this book is about getting organized and we also know that other people may be necessary in this journey. It may be the man or woman at the home improvement store (e.g. Ace, Home Depot, Menard's Lowe's) your spouse, child or therapist. Clear communication of expectations helps set boundaries, build trust, and fosters mutual understanding.

- **Shape your beliefs**: Expectations have a self-fulfilling prophecy effect. If you believe you can get this done, you're more likely to put in the effort and take the actions necessary to stay the course. On the other hand, negative expectations can become a barrier to your achievement.

Summary of Expectations

Our expectations influence our outcomes. By setting realistic and positive expectations, we can navigate through this journey more effectively and strive for personal growth and success. No matter which service or services you've chosen from the list, I'm confident that you'll gather valuable insights to enrich your organizational journey. The checklist serves as a tool for you to pinpoint exactly what you need and to establish a solid foundation for guiding your specific path. It's all about tapping into your specific expectations and using that checklist and the other valuable information as a personalized guide to enhance your progress.

THE LOOK OF ORGANIZATION

The desire for organization varies from person to person. For some, it's about getting a single space or room in order, while others aim for a complete home overhaul. Then there are those who simply crave a refrigerator that's visually pleasing, saying, "I want my refrigerator to have that celebrity touch." Additionally, some seek inspiration from friends or associates who they admire. For some it may just be social media influencers, envisioning their spaces to reflect the aesthetic allure seen on various social media platforms. On the flip side, others dream of an organized home office or a closet that makes them feel at peace. It may be your family room, living room, kitchen, vanity or basement. Whatever it is that you envision, it can be crafted. The perfect organizational plan tailored to your unique style and needs is waiting for you.

Everyone doesn't get to experience the joy of dealing with clutter, right? It's kind of funny, actually. In my line of work, I come across a lot of people who definitely do. What's really interesting is that everyone's clutter is so unique, just like they are. I'm not saying there aren't similarities among clients, because there definitely are. You've got folks with overflowing closets full of clothes or shoes, or maybe a dresser covered with perfume or cologne. Then there are the collectors—whether it's mugs, hoodies, make-up, dolls, quilts, tools, books, sunglasses, art, you name it. I have an uncle who collects cars. I too have been guilty of a couple in the past. The thing is, you have to understand your situation. You see, our possessions hold personal significance, so sorting through them becomes the real journey. Just knowing can be a quest for the peace we're all seeking.

Clutter often serves as a security blanket, providing a sense of comfort and familiarity in our surroundings. It's like those old friends we can rely on. However, it's essential to recognize that clutter can also be a coping mechanism for dealing with emotional pain or trauma. By surrounding ourselves with physical chaos, we can distract ourselves from underlying issues we may not be ready to confront.

Moreover, clutter isn't solely about emotional baggage. It can also stem from practical factors like work avoidance or a lack of proper organization systems. In educational settings, for instance, students may use restroom breaks or requests for water as a means to avoid independent work, highlighting the need for extra support, structure and/or routine.

Ultimately, tackling clutter requires addressing both the emotional and practical aspects. By acknowledging the role clutter plays in our lives and implementing effective organizational strategies, we can create environments that promote clarity, productivity, and well-being. The things that we possess need order. Giving that item order, gives you order. But everyone's order will not look the same. Surprisingly, everyone doesn't love chocolate. Can you believe that? So, it's important to understand that the sense of order we crave might not match up with what our neighbors desire or that social media influencer. We all operate in unique ways, right? What works for one person might not work for another, and that's perfectly okay. It's all about finding what resonates with us individually and embracing that diversity. After all, it's what makes life interesting, right? So, let's celebrate our individuality and preferences when it comes to organizing our spaces.

HELPFUL HINT

You must know that organizing is tailored to your specific needs. Throughout this process, you will recognize the value of each possession.

IMPACT OF CLUTTER

Being unorganized can make life tough in so many ways. When you are lacking a certain amount of order or the order that you desire in your life, it can cause unsightly clutter and/or make it difficult to find things. In an article for The Journal of Neuroscience, a team of researchers from the Princeton University Neuroscience Institute shared findings from their study on organized and cluttered living.

The researchers discovered that when there was too much stuff in sight, people had a significantly and measurably more difficult time being productive. This translates into lower levels of productivity and even more clutter.

I know from working with my clients that the lack of organization in your home can cause an unending, overall sense of anxiety or stress. Although there are some people who believe that having a neat home isn't one of the more important aspects of life, I believe differently. My reality is that your spirits can be lifted by having a certain amount of order in your space, your residence. And of course cleanliness matters, too.

For years, I had a cleaning service, and witnessing my clients' reactions upon completing a job was a remarkable feeling. As I was leaving and they were entering their homes, it was truly rewarding to see the happiness reflected in their bright smiles which validated the impact of my work and the power of a clean and organized space. I knew it made a significant difference in their lives. As they stepped into their clean and organized homes, a transformation occurred. The shift in their body language was noticeable; some would confidently flop onto the couch, feeling like they'd entered an entirely new space, feeling a sense of freedom.

Their houses, now clean and neat, became a source of empowerment for them. Clients would express their excitement to cook dinner, watch TV, and, in some cases, even offer me a friendly adult beverage. I'd overhear them on the phone proudly describing the cleanliness of their home, exuding confidence and walking around with a newfound sense of conviction. It was more than just a cleaning service; it was about creating an environment that uplifted and empowered them.

Back in those days, I had no clue I was essentially an organizer and coach. To be honest, I didn't even know what an organizer was. So, my clients were getting a three-for-one deal – not just a clean home but also some impromptu home organization and coaching thrown into the mix.

Witnessing countless faces light up with joy upon entering a space that's not just clean, but also meticulously organized is simply priceless. Reflecting on my own experiences, that amazing sense of relief when every single thing is in the rightful place and well-managed is a feeling I know and appreciate. Seeing those reactions of positive vibes warmed my heart. The surprised faces when stepping into a clean and organized environment are scenarios I've come across frequently. I can identify with that sigh of relief when your belongings aren't just managed, and also organized in a way that fits into your lifestyle.

Here's the interesting part: All of those feel-good vibes when I had my cleaning business were achieved without the hassle of moving or splurging on new furniture and accessories. That's why this process can be so fascinating.

Your Mood is a Reflection

The ambiance and vibe of your home truly shape your overall well-being. It might surprise you, but it's not just about the furniture or decor styles – what really makes a difference is the cleanliness, order, and organization in your space. As I mentioned earlier, those clients were completely satisfied with everything they already had; no one felt the need to go shopping. It was simply about having a clean and organized living space that brought them happiness.

If you've had a hard day at work and return to a home that's disorganized and needs a good cleaning, your spirits will lag. Similar to my previous cleaning clients, if you return to a home that's organized and clean, your spirits can be instantly lifted simply by walking in the door. The same applies when entering an office space and even your vehicle. You may know the feeling I'm talking about when you get a car wash, riding down the street shiny.

You can achieve a feeling of pure relaxation and contentment by making small changes in your home. Just like the client who flopped on the couch to watch TV after coming into a clean and organized space, you can achieve that feeling too.

- If you're calm and relaxed by nature, the arrangement, organization, and cleanliness of your home most likely presents serenity and peacefulness.

- If you're emotionally overwrought or plagued with anxiety or depression, your home may be cluttered, disorganized or in need of a good cleaning.

Your home or residence may be a reflection of your emotional state. Not only does the state of your home influence your mood, but the inverse is also true, according to some mental health experts. Studies indicate that how you handle your possessions in your home is a reflection of what you believe about yourself and how you feel.

If you're feeling a bit low and your living space is anything but tidy or clean, keep in mind that addressing those home challenges can actually do wonders for your emotional well-being. I've witnessed it happen countless times – the improvement can be quite significant and, at times, almost instantaneous. You just have to be clear on what you want.

HELPFUL HINT:

What you desire is attainable. Just be real with yourself and clear on what you want because you can achieve it.

Understanding MY Desire

First know that a desire is a strong feeling of wanting to have or achieve something. It's often coupled with a sense of longing or yearning. It can range from simple wishes or preferences to deep-seated aspirations and ambitions. Desires can be driven by many factors, including personal needs, societal influences, emotional impulses, or intrinsic motivations. They play a significant role in shaping human behavior, driving us to pursue goals, make decisions, and seek fulfillment in life.

Let's focus on the intrinsic motivations to execute our organizational goals. What you desire will be the driving force behind your actions. Focusing on intrinsic motivations can be a powerful driver for executing organizational goals. Intrinsic motivations refer to those internal factors that come from within us, such as personal growth, autonomy, mastery, and a sense of purpose. When we are intrinsically motivated, we are more likely to be engaged, committed, and productive in our work. It'll be the thing that helps you shape your goals and make them a reality. So, don't hold back. Dream realistically big and go after what you really want. I say realistically big because this plan needs to begin now. Begin putting things in action. When you keep it real, you can execute in the now. You've got this!

Desire Example #1

I got a call from a middle-aged couple who are constantly on the go. Setting up a consultation wasn't an immediate thing because their lives revolve around constant travel, numerous business meetings, galas, and lots of social events. Like so many, they were so caught up in their busy schedules that they'd ended up neglecting spending time with other family members. Juggling multiple businesses, they simply hadn't found the time to tend to their home the way they'd like. The impact? Well, no one would ever guess the chaos they'd navigate through in their condo.

You see, they had this desire for their home life to mirror the success they'd achieved in their businesses. They firmly believed that by getting their home more organized, they could carve out some much-needed quality time with their family. It hit them hard, coming home to chaos day in and day after a long day's work. In fear of anyone seeing this including a cleaning service, they were dead set on making a shift. Needless to say, I was more than excited to jump in and assist.

This scenario is pretty common, and many people find themselves facing this challenge. The thing is, there's a mismatch going on. That's what I call it.

Their home life doesn't quite align with the success they've achieved in their business. Now, some might argue that they live in a gorgeous home – and it is, with beautiful furniture that they absolutely love. Yet, in their eyes, the way that they have to navigate through clutter and lost time from searching for little things just doesn't match up with the way they are perceived by others. The missing link? Well, they didn't have the systems in place to maintain order.

> *I believe that with organization, you can be more successful. Finding the right balance is the key.*

Desire Example #2

I had the pleasure of working with this awesome single lady – big shoutout to all the single ladies out there! This particular lady was a shopaholic, and naturally, her wardrobe had an impressive collection of clothes and shoes. I mean, why not, right? On top of that, she had a demanding job with a lengthy commute, leaving her utterly exhausted by the time she got home. All she wanted to do was collapse, not just from fatigue but also from the overwhelm of staring at all of her stuff. The challenge? Figuring out how and where to store it all.

She tried the usual solutions – new bins and extra hangers – but it just didn't click. Accessing her things quickly and efficiently became a real struggle. At one point, she even contemplated moving into a larger house, thinking it might solve the problem.

> *Turns out, that wasn't the answer. She needed to downsize a little and some fresh ideas on how to store her beautiful clothes.*

Desire Example #3

There was this guy who wanted to bring me on board. When we had our consultation, he shared with me how challenging it was for him to get organized. He opened up about constantly feeling rushed, almost being late for work a few times. Even though he was good at what he does at work, the issue for him was not having all the tools necessary to get organized. Acknowledging his situation, he reached out to me, explaining that he dealt with executive functioning deficits. Recognizing my expertise with learning behaviors, he believed I could be the support he was seeking. The good news is, he got organized and was able to sustain organization.

Executive functioning challenges refer to difficulties in the cognitive processes that allow people to manage, and organize their thoughts and actions to achieve goals. These challenges can manifest in various areas, including time-management, focus and decision-making.

A lot of his support came from implementing strategies for time management, and utilizing tools such as planners and reminders to help him stay on track. Additionally, we worked on breaking tasks down into smaller, more manageable steps, prioritizing them based on importance and deadlines. Through consistent practice and reinforcement of these strategies, he was able to improve his executive functioning skills and maintain a higher level of organization in his personal and professional life. Our collaboration not only helped him overcome his challenges but also boosted his confidence and productivity. He's now thriving in his work and feeling more in control of his time and responsibilities.

Summary of Desire Examples

I am happy to report that the individuals that I mentioned received the order that they yearned. That couple now has systems in place and the order that they desired. I check in on them regularly. They often host dinner parties with friends and family. That single lady was able to stay in her home and we worked together to find homes for all of the belongings that she decided to keep. I was able to coach her and she has established some new routines and habits when shopping.

Setting goals with intention is a powerful way to align our desires with our actions and ultimately achieve the order we seek in our lives. Each of us has unique desires and aspirations, so it's super important to set goals that resonate with our individual lifestyles and priorities. When we do this, it can be life-altering.

Taking the time to sit down and reflect on what we truly want to accomplish in our spaces is a valuable exercise. By clarifying our intentions and identifying specific objectives, we can create a guide for achieving the order we desire. Whether it's decluttering a room, implementing an organizational system, or creating a more peaceful environment, setting clear and meaningful goals can guide our efforts and keep us focused on what truly matters. So, let's take that moment to pause, reflect, and envision the kind of space we want to inhabit. With intentional goal-setting, we can take meaningful steps toward creating a space that reflects our values, supports our well-being, and brings us fulfillment allowing us to thrive.

You've already started assessing your organizational needs with the baseline survey and by sharing other reflective responses. Recall the areas that are causing you the most stress or frustration? Tap into what you truly desire. Your vision matters. Don't just think about what you think you should want—dig deep and figure out what will truly make you happy and fulfilled in your space.

Consider Your House Matching What You Desire

Some people prefer kitchen appliances all made by the same company that coordinate with their decor. I've seen it done and it looks phenomenal! For me, it's not just about matching appliances; I want my home to be in sync with my desires, meaning that I want a sense of tranquility when I wake up every single morning. It's a tribute to the years of hard work I've put in—I aim for my space to be a living reflection of my journey. When I wake up, I want to be greeted with a sense of honor and appreciation, a daily affirmation of the effort and dedication I've poured into creating a home that resonates with peace and fulfillment. I simply want to move with ease throughout my space. You may feel the same way and if you do, you deserve it.

For some, it's about having a designated spot for a particular item(s). Some want things neatly organized in charming acrylic containers. Others want bins or baskets with labels for easy identification. Then there are those dreaming of a colossal, color-coded closet, perhaps one that effortlessly rotates with a click, revealing the perfect outfit for the day. There are those who simply say, "I just want to walk into a clean house when I get home."

Do you want a more minimalist approach, preferring to keep only essential items and declutter regularly? It ultimately depends on your preferences and organizational styles. The key is to find a system that works best for your needs and helps you maintain order and efficiency in your space.

What's your vision for your space?

What specific order do you yearn for in your space?

Close your eyes for a moment and think about your vision.

Whether it's through designated spots, containers, labels, or minimalism, the goal is to create a system that is sustainable and easy to maintain over time.

Experimenting with different methods and adapting them as needed can help find the most effective organizational strategy for your lifestyle.

Each person has their own unique design vision they aspire to achieve. For most of us, the dream is a functional and well-organized space that brings the peace of mind we crave. Creating this environment will allow inner peace, empowering you to pursue and possibly achieve anything you set your mind to do.

Our homes don't have to be dictators; they can transform into whatever we desire. Your home can reflect your aspirations and accomplishments. If you're a goal-getter, there's no need to return to a space that doesn't match what you've achieved or plan to achieve. Why settle for a home that depletes us mentally or physically when it can be a source of rejuvenation and inspiration? Curate a space that mirrors your goals and uplifts your spirits. Whatever your desire, let's bring that vision to life and create a space that resonates with your unique style and preferences.

"The need for change bulldozed a road down the center of my mind."

—Maya Angelou

WHAT DO YOU WANT TO FEEL WHEN YOU ENTER YOUR SPACE?

Use the space below to respond.

"*Whatever is bringing you down, get rid of it because you'll find that when you're free... your true self comes out.*"

—**Tina Turner**

CHAPTER 2

Order is Possible

So often we think we need to hire a junk removal company, or think that we need to move somewhere with more space. Some people do need these things, but on the other hand, many of us don't. Most of us want to see our clutter be erased with a magic wand, but think about it, the clutter didn't get there overnight. Clutter happens over a period of time. It is a collection of items. As a matter of fact, according to the Merriam-Webster Dictionary, clutter is a crowded or confused mass or collection.

According to me, these are items that no longer belong in our lives or items that simply need to be categorized in a way conducive to our lifestyles. You have to know that clutter isn't just about our surroundings. Clutter and disorganization can seep into every aspect of our lives. Our behavior can start to suffer, and our relationships can take a hit too.

Also know this—research backs up what I'm saying. Clutter and disorganization have a cumulative effect on our brains. So, the longer we let things pile up, the more it messes with our heads. Literally. So, it's time to take action because order IS possible. Being clear on your stance matters. What questions do you have about clutter? Please respond to the following:

CLUTTER QUESTIONS

1. Does clutter or dirt around the house nag at you mentally? How does clutter impact your mental state and decision-making processes?

2. Do your belongings add item after item or task after task to your to-do list? Explain.

3. Do you feel like it's impossible or difficult for you to get out of this rut?

4. Do you yearn for a more sustainable living environment? Explain.

5. Have you ever noticed how much more relaxed you feel when you come home to a clean and organized house? Explain.

Use figurative language or figurative speech to describe
an excessive amount of belongings?

"*The thing that creates clutter
can feel like a friend and then
you realize it's an enemy waiting
for its destiny which is ultimately
your destiny.*"
—**Sylvia Holloway**

SIFTING IS YOUR FRIEND

Alright, this is when we learn the true power of evaluating our belongings and it starts with sifting. I'm not talking about flour. I'm talking about taking the time to go through your stuff and figuring out what really matters. That's key, no matter how cluttered—or not—your space may be. It's like a yearly check-up for your belongings, and trust me, it's worth the effort.

I know, I know, the thought of sifting through everything can seem daunting. I get it. The idea of sifting through all your stuff can be an annoying task. But trust me when I say this—it's an extremely important task for setting up a well-organized system that works for you.

Let me share a little insight from my experience with clients. Many of them have expressed the urge to just toss everything out and start fresh. But here's the thing: when we actually took the time to sift through their belongings, we often stumbled upon time sensitive documents, financial statements, IDs, or checks—these are some of the essential things they were on the verge of discarding.

And here's the real tea: some of this stuff can't just be thrown in the trash. Certain items need to be handled carefully, shredded, or disposed of in specific ways to protect your privacy and security. So, my advice? Sift through your belongings wisely. Take your time, and don't be too hasty to toss things out. You never know what valuable items or important documents you might uncover in the process. Trust me, it's worth the effort.

At times, the impulse might be to declutter by getting rid of everything and starting fresh. While that might initially sound appealing, it might not be the best course of action. After all, every item in our possession was acquired for a reason, and each piece in our home was chosen with purpose. So sift and sift wisely. When it's that time, grab some boxes, put on your favorite playlist, and just start sifting wisely.

To guide you through this sifting process, consider the following questions. They will help you discern what items are worth holding onto and what can be let go:

1. *What items are necessary for me to function?*

_____

_____

2. *What items are necessary for me to thrive?*

_____

_____

3. *Which items are going to support me in getting me to the level I want to be in my life?*

_____

_____

Also ask yourself, **"Which items are hindering me?"** What items are actually holding me back? Yes, ask yourself, **"What items are in my way? Which items are not matching the path that I have created or would like to create for myself?"**

HELPFUL HINT:

We have to answer questions that can sometimes appear to be tough because these are the questions that we're going to use to determine what really needs to stay in our lives and what is hindering us and must go.

MORE SIFTING QUESTIONS

Certain words are **bolded** and underlined. As you sift, feel free to substitute the bolded words to what you come across on your path.

- Do I really need all of these **jeans**?

- Why did I even buy this **candle**?

- Do I need 100 pairs of **earrings**?

- Why do I keep all of these **hair products** that aren't making a difference?

- How long do I keep these **tax papers**?

- Do I need all of these **bracelets**?

- When was the last time I carried this **clutch bag**, or wore this hat?

- Is **the heel on these shoes** still in style?

That list can go on and on if you think about it. I know that some of those questions may appear to be silly, but when we have an abundance of things and lack storage for those items, it becomes a problem. If items are not quickly accessible, that too can be a problem. If I need scissors, I want them now. If I'm being audited and need paperwork from two or three years ago, I need it now. It shouldn't be a whole production for me to access what I need to get. Our time is way too precious.

I understand that you may want to keep things like your yearbook, childhood photos, your cap and gown. There is a place for sentimental items and everything else you own. You may not need to keep everything that you own. There may only be one item that you part with or 100 items. And please don't mistake this process for a throw away session. Sifting is like a check-in session with what you own.

YOU HAVE TO KNOW

What you keep and what you don't keep is to be determined by you because you know what you want to live with and how you feel about what you choose to keep. Whatever you keep has to be properly stored. Yes, everything you keep has to be stored somewhere.

THE POWER OF SORT AND STORE

To have a neater home, sort and store your possessions in an organized fashion. What do I mean by organized fashion? I mean, in an organized way. How are you assigning homes to your belongings? Let me share some examples:

T-Shirts: If you wear logo T-shirts like me and I mean a lot of logo T-Shirts, you can create a space for them. I have a drawer dedicated to logo T-Shirts. This is how I fold them:

1. Lay your shirt flat on a solid surface, with the front side facing down.

2. Smooth out any little creases, ensuring a clean fold.

3. Fold the sleeves over, crossing them across the back of the shirt. Nice and crisp.

4. Next, fold each side of the T-shirt towards the center, creating a tidy rectangle.

5. Now, fold the T-shirt in half so that the front of the top is facing upwards.

6. If you're dealing with adult-sized T-shirts, take it a step further: fold the T-shirt into thirds, with the bottom section folding over the middle, then the top section folding over that. This achieves the same polished finish.

Organization or Company Apparel: If you belong to a special organization or have to wear company shirts to the functions, group those shirts together in your closet or in a drawer depending on how many you have. If it's just a few items, you can combine it with something similar. A lot of my clients are in sororities and they have specific colors. I group those items together so they can be easily accessed for meetings or other activities.

Dresses/Suits: For special ceremonies where a specific color dress or suit is required, it's beneficial to designate a section in the closet specifically for formal items. I often advise clients to group these together, ensuring easy access when needed. Additionally, I recommend hanging longer items in a way that avoids stacking them on top of each other, such as using hangers with adequate space below, to prevent wrinkling before wearing the garment.

Keys: Having an organized home simply means you can lay your hands on things when and where you need them. Don't make this difficult, really. Take keys, for instance—just keep them near the door or toss them in a little bowl on a shelf. You could even purchase a hook for that one special key. If you're renting or prefer to keep things hole-free, there are plenty of options out there, like Command hooks or similar brands, that'll do the trick without leaving a mark. You've got this!

Garage Opener: One of my client's places their garage opener on the top shelf of the bookcase in their family room. They do that because that is the first room they enter when coming out of the garage and they don't want anyone in the family to accidentally touch it and have their garage going up without their knowledge.

HELPFUL HINT:

Everything you keep has to be stored somewhere. When organizing, make your items accessible and convenient for you.

I've heard people say that the worst part about organizing your life is that it seems like it can take a lot of time. Some people get overwhelmed by the mere thought of it all. That's one reason why so many people struggle to get organized and to find organizational strategies that are tailored to specific needs.

THINK ABOUT THIS

Individuals who view organizing as time-consuming often fail to realize its manageability when compared to the multitude of tasks they tackle daily. From managing substantial businesses to nurturing relationships, pursuing degrees, or raising children, these endeavors demand significant time investments.

It's essential to acknowledge that any meaningful improvement in life, whether personal or professional, inherently demands dedicated time and effort. However, it doesn't have to take much time at all! The strategy is to work it into your life in ways that don't take so much time.

HELPFUL TIP:

Once you create a habit and create a place for all the items, it won't appear as work. It will actually be fun because progress is so exciting!

A PLACE FOR EVERYTHING

Certain items in our daily lives are like our sidekicks, always there when we need them. They're the essentials, and they need to be within arm's reach. I vividly remember my very first cleaning client, Rosalyn, affectionately remarking to one of my sisters that I've created a "farm" for everything in her house. She'd playfully say, "Let me go to my pen farm," finding humor in how I categorize her belongings.

As a professional organizer, my approach goes beyond just putting things together; it involves ensuring that every item has a designated and accessible spot. For Rosalyn, and for anyone seeking a more organized living space, it's not just about grouping items but also about making them aware of where everything resides. I consistently experimented with new arrangements to guarantee accessibility and convenience for her.

The key is to establish a permanent home for your belongings. Your things, your daily necessities, should effortlessly integrate into your living space, always being at your fingertips. That's not saying that they have to be visible, but wherever it is, make sure it's not a struggle to access. By creating designated spaces, you not only ensure accessibility but also bring a sense of order to your home. It's about making your surroundings work for you, and in doing so, you enhance both functionality and comfortably.

"I'm so obsessed with having access to the things that I need."
—**Sylvia Holloway**

Childhood Story

Growing up, my mother had this huge white Bible that served a dual purpose - it was both a decorative piece in our living room and an unsuspecting storage hub for our most vital documents. Social security cards and birth certificates were within its pages, forming an unconventional yet steadfast repository. It was a fixture in our home, and no one dared to touch it.

In retrospect, stashing such critical documents in a Bible may not have been the most secure choice, but it worked for us. It became the go-to spot for retrieving essential information. When the time came for my first visit to the DMV for a driver's license, I knew exactly where to find my pertinent documents - in the white Bible. Witnessing my father reaching for the Bible signaled that he was likely in the process of renewing his license. It became our family's permanent home for those personal documents.

Designated Areas

This concept of having a designated place for important items extends beyond documents. If you're someone who takes copious notes, having a dedicated spot for your journal, whether it's in your desk drawer or near your computer, ensures that your thoughts and ideas are always within arm's reach. This practice not only contributes to a sense of organization, but also saves valuable time when you need to reference or jot down something important.

Navigating the realms of organization, be it in your workspace or your living area, always circles back to a fundamental principle that everything should have a designated place where it "lives." Let's delve into this concept by considering a humble example: tape. Even the smallest items, like tape, deserve their own home or farm, be it a designated box or a drawer.

This notion extends beyond just small items; it encompasses everything in your surroundings. The key lies in establishing predetermined homes for each item. Imagine a world where every pen, paperclip, or cherished memento has a spot to call its own. This isn't just about maintaining an organized environment; it's about living peacefully.

Living in a digital world certainly offers convenience, but it also introduces its own challenges. While many documents, like insurance cards, are now digital, relying solely on digital copies can pose risks, such as the possibility of your phone running out of energy when needed most. In such situations, having physical paper copies becomes necessary. So, where do you keep all these important documents? Have you discussed this with your family? It's a valid question that requires thoughtful consideration and a reliable storage solution.

* _____ Vehicle Insurance

* _____ Home Insurance

* _____ Life Insurance

* _____ Spare Car Keys

* _____ Birth Certificate

* _____ Social Security Card

* _____ Passport

* _____ Other

When You Know, You know

When every item knows its place, you have created a space of order. No longer will items wander aimlessly, causing a scavenger hunt when it's time to access it. The perpetual game of hide-and-seek is replaced with a sense of predictability.

* **Need the scissors?** Check the drawer.

* **Need the password?** Check the safe.

* **Looking for insurance papers?** It's safely tucked in the labeled folder.

Moreover, this meticulous placement isn't just about preventing the frustration of misplaced items; it's a defense mechanism against the encroachment of clutter. Items with designated homes aren't likely to contribute to the chaos that can gradually pervade your space.

Think of it as a proactive defense against clutter before it even has a chance to settle in. Embrace meticulous placement. So, as you continue on the journey of organization, remember the golden rule - assign a home for everything. Even the seemingly inconspicuous items like tape, safety pins, and paperclips will be in a designated area. Grouping items creates order, contributing to a space that is not only visually pleasing, but also inherently functional. What are the benefits of all of this detail? Well, there are so many benefits and establishing order simply sets you up for success, allowing you to thrive.

- **How can I become more efficient? How does maintaining organization contribute to improving my efficiency?**

  Take some time to really consider your options when it comes to making sure that everything has a place on a permanent basis. Having a designated place for everything holds benefits. Knowing where your things are located allows your day to flow, daily tasks, reducing time spent searching for what you need to be successful. This efficiency leads to increased productivity, which will allow you to focus on goals and other cool stuff that you like to do or always wanted to do.

- **How can my stress be reduced as it relates to being organized?**

  When things aren't put away, it causes clutter and clutter can sometimes cause you stress. Having a designated place for each item creates a visually organized and calming environment, promoting order and control. Being organized can reduce stress and anxiety.

- **How can I use my time more effectively? How can being organized improve my time management?**

Time management is essential, and establishing routines and structures can significantly enhance productivity and goal achievement. By incorporating dedicated time for tasks like returning items to their designated places, you maximize efficiency and reduce clutter, ultimately creating a productive environment. While spontaneity adds a touch of excitement to life, having a prioritized schedule ensures that essential tasks are completed, leading to personal fulfillment and a balanced life. This structured approach not only benefits you, but also positively impacts your loved ones, which contributes to a thriving lifestyle.

- **How can being organized enhance my focus?**

An organized space can minimize distractions. Have you ever been to a restaurant and had to tell the waiter or waitress to clean the table? I have. I wouldn't have been able to have dinner or lunch at a table that wasn't clean to my liking. That's distracting. Clean and organized environments are important because it allows you to focus. When you sit down to do work, you don't want to have to keep thinking clutter or about when you finish with your deadline that you have to sort through everything on your desk or dining room table.

- **How can implementing organizational strategies enhance my financial situation?**

When you're organized, you can easily access critical documents as needed. Have you ever found yourself purchasing something only to realize later that you already had it at home? Whether it's buying new underwear due to a lack of laundry or scrambling to find an outfit for an event because your preferred choice was at the cleaners, these situations can be frustrating. Establishing habits and knowing the location of your belongings can help prevent the need for unnecessary repurchases.

This also has a lot to do with implementing schedules and routines. I'm no financial guru, but Arthur Anderson of the Anderson Ace System shared,

"Having a well-structured system for managing finances can help prevent late fees on overdue bills, provide clarity on spending and savings objectives."

- **How can organization promote healthy habits?**

Once more, it all circles back to the concept of schedules. When we establish a routine that includes regular exercise, it becomes challenging to deviate from it because we've ingrained it as a habit.

Personally, I don't like crowded grocery stores. I've established a specific time for my grocery shopping to ensure a hassle-free experience. Choosing a less crowded period allows me to quickly pick up the ingredients and snacks I enjoy for the week. These snacks are not only healthy but also easy for me to grab and eat on the go.

Organized spaces can foster healthier habits, having a designated area for work can inspire your creative juices to flow. Similarly, a well-organized bedroom contributes to promoting healthy sleep habits and we know how important sleep is for our health.

- **How will organization improve my mental well-being?**

Improving your mental well-being is essential, and creating a conducive environment plays a significant role in achieving this. By consciously cultivating a mood or vibe that aligns with the mindset you wish to adopt, you can positively impact your mental health. An organized environment, in particular, can have a profound effect by instilling a sense of order and control in your life. This reduction in chaos and overwhelm contributes to a more positive mindset, fostering greater emotional stability and well-being.

- **How can being organized improve my relationships?**

I don't know if you share a bedroom or bathroom with someone, but if you do, having a designated place for your items is crucial. Shared spaces such as bathrooms, bedrooms, and work spaces, benefit from organization. This will help to minimize potential conflicts over misplaced items and not so tidy areas. *This is relevant in various settings, rather it be personal (at home) or professional (at work). This will allow you to foster fluid collaborations and healthier relationships.*

- **Can being organized improve my creativity?**

   Absolutely! When you're looking to tap into your creative juices and boost productivity, an organized space is key. It creates an environment that welcomes inspiration and focus, allowing your mind to think more clearly and creatively. By eliminating unnecessary distractions like clutter, you free up mental space to explore new ideas, solve problems, and unleash your creativity to its maximum potential.

   In essence, having a place for everything that you own contributes to a more structured, efficient, and fulfilling lifestyle. This will positively influence various aspects of your life and will ultimately allow you to thrive. Having a place for all of your belongings will also contribute to a sense of confidence and greater appreciation for what you own.

   HELPFUL HINT/PRO TIP:

   Testing out strategies to find what works for you will be a systematic and reflective approach.

I had to learn to reevaluate everything that I brought into my space.
It's actually a form of self-care and me being responsible.

"*Everything that you elect to keep, has to be stored. Everytime you make a purchase, no matter how big or small, it will need to be stored somewhere.*"
—**Sylvia Holloway**

CREATE HOMES

Let's take a moment to reflect on where our belongings currently reside and how well our current systems are working for us. Consider the following questions, either by jotting down your responses or contemplating silently:

1. **Where do you keep your car keys?**

    Are they hanging by the door, tucked into a specific pocket, or maybe resting in a designated bowl? Visualize the spot you've chosen and assess whether it's a convenient and easily accessible location.

2. **Where do you keep your stamps?**

Are they stashed away in a desk drawer, neatly organized in a designated container, or perhaps residing in a catch-all drawer? Reflect on the accessibility of your chosen spot and whether it aligns with your stamp-related activities.

3. **Where do you keep your mail?**

Take a moment to reflect on where you currently keep your incoming mail: Is it neatly organized in a designated mail sorter, filed away in a meticulously labeled folder, or perhaps scattered in various places throughout your living space? Consider the efficiency of your current mail storage arrangement.

4. **Where do you keep your tax papers?**

    Are they filed away in a meticulously labeled folder, stored in a designated box, or scattered in various places? Consider the efficiency of your current arrangement.

5. **Where do you typically enjoy your meals?** Is it in the desired spot you envisioned for mealtime? Do you find yourself eating in front of the TV?

   Take a moment to reflect – is this arrangement working for you? Would you change anything about where you usually eat, and why or why not? It's worth considering how your dining setup aligns with your lifestyle and preferences.

6. **What's your system for paying bills?**

How do you currently tackle this task? Is it a smooth sailing, stress-free process, or do you find yourself wishing for a change? Would you like to tweak anything about how you handle your bills? Maybe it's the organization of the paperwork, the digital system you use, or the overall efficiency of the process. Share your thoughts – what aspects are working seamlessly, and where do you see room for improvement?

After talking about bills, we (me and you) may need a little breather so let's bring it down a notch. Let's think of an item that often finds its way into our homes like gift bags. Take a moment to reflect on where you currently keep your collection of gift bags. Are they neatly filed away in a meticulously labeled folder, organized in a designated box, or scattered in various places throughout your space?

Consider the efficiency of your existing arrangement. Are your gift bags easily accessible when your friend or family member has a special celebration or do you find yourself rummaging through different areas in search of the perfect bag for a special occasion? Assessing how and where you store your gift bags allows you to gauge the effectiveness of your current system.

Just like tax documents, gift bags serve a purpose and are often needed at specific times. Having a designated and easily accessible space for them not only prevents you from searching when the occasion calls for it, but also contributes to the overall organization of your living space.

So, where do you keep your gift bags, and does their current home align with the convenience you desire? Can you tell that gift bags are a *thing* where I live? Whether it's gift bags, wrapping paper, hair products, make-up. golf balls, cleaning products, or dish towels, taking a moment to evaluate and potentially refine this aspect of your organization can bring both practicality and order to your home. Examine your current set-up and find a system that works for you and stick to it. There are many different organizational methods that you can choose to implement, but the most important element is to use it consistently. Make sure you understand it and follow through.

For example, there are different ways you can organize your bookshelf. You can put your books in order by author, color, or by topic. Choose a system that aligns with your lifestyle. The last thing you need is to be scrambling for an item and now you have items scattered everywhere because it wasn't easily accessible for you. Once you choose a system, all you need to worry about is following through.

By examining your specific items and where they "live" in your daily life, you gain insights into the effectiveness of your organizational systems. Look at how you move. Think about your schedule, the flow of your day. Those are your current habits and setups. This awareness becomes the foundation for making intentional choices about where items should ideally reside to enhance accessibility, reduce frustration, and contribute to an overall sense of order in your space.

As you find homes or "farms" as my client Rosalyn jokingly referred to her items, you'll need to identify the most effective methods tailored to your individual needs and organizational goals. You know if an item needs a home because these items may be scattered throughout your space or some may be hidden somewhere like in a junk drawer. Find a designated area for all of your items. Create a list of items that need to be stored.

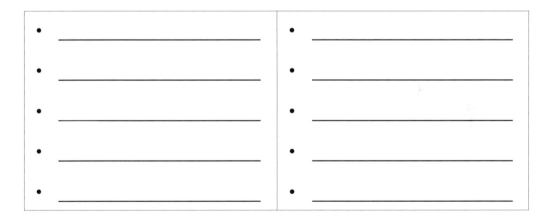

Jump into your own personal research. Using the information acquired from this book, talking to friends, or getting insights from family members, uncover strategies that have worked for them. Let's say that you never know what to do with the plastic containers that you get from take out at restaurants. *No, that's*

too easy because you can wash them and recycle them, especially if you have a set of plastic containers that you regularly use. Anyway, it's all about gathering a variety of perspectives and methodologies so you can create a diverse pool of options that will align with your unique lifestyle.

As you compile this information, prioritize these strategies based on their relevance to your organizational goals, and your own personal preferences. Reflect on what resonates with you, considering the practical aspects that align with your daily routine and preferences. For instance, I enjoy grocery shopping, but I don't like waiting in long lines. I've found that avoiding crowded grocery store trips enhances my overall well-being. Choosing a specific day and time for grocery shopping ensures a constant supply of healthy food options while keeping my mind at ease.

Now, let's expand on potential strategies that might resonate with you. Perhaps designating specific days for certain activities can provide a structured routine. Or, consider creating designated spaces for commonly used items. Ultimately, the goal is to tailor these strategies to your lifestyle, creating a personalized toolkit that enhances your organizational prowess. By embracing diverse perspectives and adapting strategies to fit your needs, you're not just organizing; you're crafting a lifestyle that integrates order and simplicity. So, with that being said, what's a system that can be improved or one that needs to be established. How could giving attention to this system buy you time or contribute to your unique journey towards a more organized and fulfilling life?

Directions: Set a timer for about 3 minutes and jot down some ideas that you are considering. Then circle 3-4 that stand out to you.

Embrace strategy. This may sound more complex than what it is, but you may just be testing out a new place to place your keys if you always misplace them in your home. You may always be on a hunt when you need a pen so this would be a great test strategy. Another strategy that can be incorporated is choosing a day to get gas so you're not stopping at some random, over priced gas station.

Starting small with strategy implementation allows you to assess how your new systems are working without feeling overwhelmed. Gradual implementation of these new strategies that you are creating for yourself will also help in identifying specific elements that contribute to success or challenges.

List 3 strategies or systems that you would like to test and briefly explain how this will impact your life.

_____
_____
_____
_____
_____
_____

_____
_____
_____
_____
_____

Be consistent. Consistency isn't just a suggestion; it's the linchpin for success as you embark on implementing and sustaining these strategies. Once you've laid out your plan, make a dedicated commitment to stick with each strategy consistently for a specified period – no shortcuts and no wavering. This commitment serves a dual purpose.

First, it ensures that you're giving each strategy a fair shake. Sometimes the real improvement happens when you persist through the initial phases, allowing the strategy to fully unfold and showcase its potential. It's like anything in life that you nurture – consistency transforms the ordinary into the extraordinary.

Second, committing to consistency provides you with the invaluable opportunity to observe the long-term effects of each strategy. It's not just about quick wins; it's about sustained progress and lasting impact. By staying the course, you become a keen observer of the shifts and improvements that occur over time. This insight guides you towards fine-tuning your approach and making informed decisions based on tangible results. Remember, it's about a lifestyle shift.

1. Monitor by regularly checking in on your progress and evaluating how well each strategy is doing the trick. Now, here's a little trick I've picked up along the way – have a conversation with yourself. Yes, you heard that right! Ask yourself the real questions: Is this strategy working for me? Is it bringing the results you're after? Are the results benefitting me?

2. Be open to making adjustments. If a particular strategy isn't yielding the desired results, you may have to tweak it or replace it with another. So you are ultimately fine-tuning. Remember, don't be afraid to make adjustments. It's like a little experiment within your own space – a trial and error that helps you figure out what truly works for you.

3. Remember, this journey is all about customization. What works for one person might need a bit of a tweak for you. So, embrace the dialogue with yourself, keep an open mind, and let the process unfold. It's not just about finding a home for your belongings; it's about creating a system that syncs with your lifestyle. So, talk it out, make those tweaks, and enjoy the evolving journey of organization. You've got this! This is self-care because these strategies are strategies that you can use forever.

4. After testing several strategies, reflect on your experiences and outcomes. Identify the strategies that consistently contribute to your success and align with your lifestyle. Choose those that you can sustain over a long period of time.

5. Recognize that finding what works for you is an ongoing process. Commit to continuous progress. Be open to trying new approaches, and adapt your strategies based on changing circumstances or goals.

Here's a pro-tip: Once you have incorporated the initial batch of three to four strategies into your routine and they feel like second nature to you, that's the cue for you to introduce more into your organizational repertoire. It's an evolving process, constantly fine-tuning your approach as you grow more adept at managing your space and time.

They say it's the little things and I believe them.

"*Sometimes it seems like the smallest things can make or break a situation, a situation that can have a huge impact on the flow of your day or the flow of your life.*"
—**Sylvia Holloway**

SYSTEMS IN MOTION

Now, let's dive into the strategies you might already have in place. Take a moment to check off those that resonate with your current routine. This isn't just about identifying what you do; it's about acknowledging and celebrating the strategies that are already part of your organizational arsenal.

Say to yourself, "I already do the following and I'm good on this," and check off the strategies that apply to you. Feel free to add to the list.

- ☐ I have a designated area for toiletries.
- ☐ I have a designated day to wash clothes.
- ☐ I make my bed every day.
- ☐ I have a storage area for cleaning supplies.
- ☐ I have a set day to go to the grocery store.
- ☐ I have a set day to review and pay bills.
- ☐ I have a set day or days to get gas.
- ☐ I schedule a time to write out my to-do list.
- ☐ I have a skin care routine.
- ☐ I have a set workout schedule.
- ☐ I schedule time to read.
- ☐ I have a scheduled time to meditate.
- ☐ I check-in on family members.
- ☐ I plan what I'm going to wear for the next day.
- ☐ I keep in contact with friends from high school.
- ☐ I pack a healthy snack or lunch.
- ☐ _____

The Bed. Making your bed every day might sound like a small feat, but trust me, it's a positivity generator. My mom, the bed-making queen, swears by it. Here's a blurb from Yolanda Malcolm, my real estate guru client – "Coming home to a well-made bed after a day of showing homes is an ultimate mood lifter."

So, if you checked off that box, you're already on the daily bed-making bandwagon and that's wonderful! You already know the magic it brings. If you haven't embraced this strategy yet, why not give it a shot? A well-made bed screams discipline and organization, setting the stage for a day where you're in control. Plus, crawling into a well-made bed at night feels so cozy.

- Making your bed daily establishes a routine and helps you embrace a more organized lifestyle. That's our goal. We are implementing new strategies and the ones that work are here to stay.

- Starting your day with your bed being made is a quick win in the morning and it sets the productivity wheels in motion as you gain confidence to handle whatever comes your way.

- The precision it takes to make your bed will pour over into other areas of your life.

- You start paying attention to details, and that will enhance your organization skills.

- Organization is about repetition. Making your bed each day is a simple, repetitive task that may put you at ease before you tackle your day.

Coming back to a well-made bed at night is necessary. The last thing you want to have to do when you are tired from a hard day is have to clear your bed or shove everything to the floor to climb in. Who wants to wake up to have to see that mess? We want to wake up in a peaceful mood.

Alright, so I've thrown a bunch of reasons your way – and I get it, it may have been a long list to emphasize one point. But here's the takeaway that's the real tea: making your bed daily has a ton of perks. It's not just about the pillows and sheets; it's about setting a tone for routine and positivity.

Now, back to the previous list, if you checked off anything on that list, high-five! You're already in motion, and that means you've got the knack for establishing routines into your life. So, here's a question: What's your next move? What new strategy do you want to give to try to amp up your life? Let's make it happen! Let's go! List 2 more strategies that you would like to test when you are ready. Briefly explain how these strategies will impact your life.

_____

_____

_____

_____

_____

_____

_____

_____

_____

_____

HELPFUL HINT:

The strategies that you are incorporating are allowing you to thrive. Keep implementing them little by little.

"Dreams are lovely but they are just dreams. Fleeting, ephemeral, pretty. But dreams do not come true just because you dream them. It's hard work that makes things happen. It's hard work that creates change."

—Shonda Rhimes

CHAPTER 3

Release

IT'S GOT TO GO

I'm genuinely passionate about recycling, and it would be fantastic if everyone could make the effort to play their part in this eco-friendly practice. However, let's face it – not everything is meant for recycling. There are certain items that, realistically, should find their way to the trash bin. It's just a reality we have to acknowledge. So, while I'm all for recycling, let's also be mindful of what truly belongs in the recycling bin and what should be responsibly disposed of elsewhere. Together, we can make a significant impact on our environment.

Here's a list of some common items that should be placed in the trash and definitely not recycled:

- **Styrofoam** can be challenging to recycle and often not accepted in curbside recycling programs.

- **Frozen Food Boxes and Pizza Boxes** with lots of grease stains or food residue are not recyclable. Remove the clean cardboard before recycling.

- **Broken Glass** is a serious safety hazard. I usually wrap it in used rags or newspapers.

- **Snotty Tissue and Paper Towels** should be thrown in the trash and items soiled with food, or liquid.

- **Disposable Diapers**

- **Old Sunblock**

- **Old makeup**

- **Personal Hygiene Products**

- **Ceramics and Pottery**

- **Batteries**

- **Electronics**

- **Light Bulbs**

- **Mirrors**

- **Electrical Cords and Hoses**

Always check with your local recycling program for specific guidelines, as recycling capabilities can vary by location. Proper disposal of items helps prevent contamination in recycling streams and ensures that recyclable materials are processed effectively. Throughout your organizational journey, you will need to make sure you donate, recycle, or throw away things that you no longer need.

PRO TIP: When you're going through your clutter, decide *immediately* whether or not you've used the item in the past couple months or years. If you haven't, consider giving it away to charity.

Always remember that your first instincts are often right. If your first instinct is to get rid of something, don't overthink it. Make a commitment on the spot. You don't want to end up keeping something that sticks around for another couple years or longer that you knew you should've parted with in the first place. The last thing you need is a house museum with a bunch of unused items!

Short story. So, my mom brought up this dress that had been hanging in my closet untouched for some time. She said, "Where's that dress of yours that you wore in Baton Rouge?" And I said, "Oh, that's on its way to be donated. It's too big." But then she said, "Keep it, you never know." In my head, I'm just thinking, "Why keep something I can't even rock?" Didn't bother arguing with her, though.

It's a really cute classic, black dress and let me be brutally honest, I don't ever want to see it in my wardrobe ever again. I can't fit it, which is a victory and it's a reminder of where I don't want to be. The lesson here is pretty straightforward: Don't cling onto the unnecessary. Life's too short to hoard stuff that doesn't serve you anymore.

Benefits of Donating

Decluttering brings about a wonderful sense of contentment, knowing that the items not actively in use could find new purpose and bring joy to someone else. It's a rewarding experience to imagine these belongings being appreciated by others in need or friends who may have had their eye on something you own.

Consider boxing up or bagging these items, including clothing, and explore opportunities to donate to your friends, family, local churches, homeless shelters, or well-known charitable organizations. By doing so, you not only create space in your life, but also contribute to making a positive impact in the lives of others. It's a win-win that adds an extra layer of fulfillment to your decluttering journey.

When the holiday season approaches, I have this little tradition where I go into my closet and pull out all those items with tags – you know, the ones that I will probably never wear or that may or may not fit me anymore. I gather these treasures, toss them into gift bags, and boom! I've inadvertently gone shopping for others within the confines of my own closet.

The satisfaction goes beyond just decluttering; it's about the positive vibes that come with giving. There's an indescribable warmth in knowing that those who might not be on my regular gift list are now recipients of these unexpected acts of kindness. It turns a simple act of cleaning out my wardrobe into a ripple of goodwill, in ways I hadn't anticipated. The holidays become a time not just for personal reflection, but also for extending that feel-good spirit to others around me.

Make a list of people who are approximately your size (clothes or shoes) or someone who may adore a thoughtful gift because trust me, that's not everyone. Check into it, they may have a special day coming up and you may have something right in your space that you can give them.

1. _____

2. _____

3. _____

4. _____

5. _____

6. _____

My Personal Donation Rule: What Would Sylvia Do?

a. My personal rule is to donate acceptable items.

b. I donate clean clothes that can actually be worn.

c. I do not donate items with holes or permanent stains (e.g., grease stains, bleach stains).

My personal thought is: If you couldn't get the stain out, chances are that the person on the receiving end won't be able to get it out either.

When clothes have permanent stains, I cut them up and use them as rags to clean around the house. Depending on the fabric, I'll use these rags for dusting, wiping up spills, washing the walls, or cleaning window ledges.

> *That cotton sundress with a barbeque stain that was stubborn can now be used to sanitize the bathroom, steps, and/or dust off my dresser. Hopefully you'll get at least a couple of years out of your favorite dress or those leggings, whatever you choose to use.*

After I use clothes as rags, I typically discard them. Here's another tip, if you find that you're accumulating too many rags, just use them immediately and discard them because the last thing you need is a bin of rags. We don't need a part two of the plastic bag saga. In my opinion, some of us have way too many plastic bags in our homes.

Say no to procrastination. Here's a pro-tip for your decluttering that's been a real help for me: Make quick moves! Whether you're tackling a massive cleanup or just clearing a small corner, the key is to get those items out of your way and quickly. No matter the size of your space-clearing mission, the fact that you've committed to it is a big win in itself.

When you've made the decision to donate, don't let them linger around in your space. Toss them straight into a bag or box and, when it's full, make a beeline for your car's trunk. Trust me, that sense of accomplishment you get when you pass by a donation site and part ways with that clutter is peaceful. I do it all the time for clients and myself and each time, it's a freeing feeling.

Picture this: the last thing you want is a donation bag lurking by the door or casually hanging out in your bedroom, waiting to trip up an unsuspecting family member. Clutter has a knack for being messy. So, don't wait until the bag is bursting at the seams; take it and get it out of your sight immediately.

HELPFUL TIP:

Once you've made up your mind to let go of something, don't second-guess it. No peeking into the bag to rescue items you've already decided must go. If it's destined for a family member or friend, hand-deliver it or ship it off if they live in another state.

The key is simple: get it out of your way, and you'll be amazed at how much smoother decluttering becomes. Cheers to you in advance for creating space and leaving the clutter behind!

Donation Sites

You can donate to your favorite charity or organization. The following places accept women's and/or men's clothes. Everything can't be donated everywhere. Donation sites usually have a specific criteria for accepting items. Surprisingly, one of the popular donation sites in my area currently does not accept:

- Chairs, stools, or couches

- Mattresses and bed frames

- Desks or other office furniture

- Tables of any kind

- Dressers, bookcases, entertainment centers, etc.

- Large exercise equipment

- Pianos

- CRT TVs

- CRT Computer Monitors

- Household chemical products: pesticides, paint, paint thinner, drain cleaner, oven cleaner, aerosols, and other environmentally unfriendly waste products.

- Personal care items such as shampoo, conditioner, nail polish remover, shaving cream, hairsprays, or shavers

- Fragrance items

In the past, where have you directed your donations, if any? Are there any new organizations or causes you're considering supporting now?

Contact donation sites in advance. Don't hesitate to call to find out what they may or may not accept. Also contact the facility that you are thinking of donating to for updated hours or times in which they accept items. Below is a list of some of some places that are exclusive to the Chicagoland area. I included them to give you examples and to include what some organizations accept. Hopefully you have a similar organization in your area.

- Savers Thrift Superstore: clothes and accessories

- The Cara Program: new/gently worn professional clothing

- Dress for Success: new/gently used in-season clothes

- Bridge to Success: clothing, accessories, and jewelry

- Pacific Garden Mission

- Midwest Veterans Closet

- Family Tree Resale

- The Self Help Closet & Pantry of Des Plaines: in-season clothing in very good condition, new underwear

- Epilepsy Foundation of Greater Chicago: bathing suits, bras, foundation garments, fur hats, nightgowns, slips, dresses, skirts, suits, bathrobes, evening dresses, fur coats, handbags, pants suits, blouses, coats, jackets, slacks, sweaters, jeans, socks, undergarments, and hats

- Illinois AMVETS

- The Sharing Connection: seasonal clothing, professional clothing, new socks, and new underwear

- Brown Elephant: apparel and handbags

- Goodwill Industries International

- Salvation Army

- American Red Cross

- Habitat for Humanity

- Feeding America

- DonorsChoose

- National Kidney Foundation

- Big Brothers Big Sisters of America:

- Good360

- Dress for Success

- Boys & Girls Clubs of America

- National Alliance on Mental Illness (NAMI)

Please note that some of the organizations mentioned may have regional variations, and it's always a good idea to check their websites or contact them directly to confirm their current donation processes and accepted items. Additionally, new organizations or changes in existing ones may have occurred since my last update.

Obtain Tax Receipt(s): Don't forget to get your tax receipt when donating items. The IRS may not check every individual donation receipt, but it's best to operate as if they do. You want to be ready if the IRS decides to check your records. Speak to your tax preparer in detail about tax questions and tax receipts.

HELPFUL TIP:

When storing receipts, I place my paper receipts in binders and folders. I have categories for receipts based on spending and I scan my receipts monthly or bi-monthly.

Time to Check-In

Let's do a mood check. Understanding your mood may help you work out what causes them and how you tend to behave when experiencing varying moods. The goal is to enhance. At this time, acknowledge your current feelings. Are they positive, negative, or a balance of both? Check the ones that apply to you at this time as it relates to your organizing journey. Feel free to add to this list.

Check-In Date: _____

❏ Ready	❏ Defeated
❏ Inadequate	❏ Anxious
❏ Overwhelmed	❏ Empowered
❏ Excited	❏ Lonely
❏ Tired	❏ Hopeful
❏ Frustrated	❏ Powerless
❏ Depressed	❏ Inspired
❏ Curious	❏ Determined
❏ Nervous	❏ Prepared
❏ Inadequate	❏ Brave
❏ Motivated	❏ Confused
❏ Intrigued	❏ Scared
❏ _____	❏ _____

Simplify

LTOY

Part Two

Getting It Done

"Just take care of one thing at a time. Do that several times and you'll notice the progress."
-Sylvia Holloway

CHAPTER 4

Self-Assessment

It's important to live comfortably in a functional space. Having a home that's comfortable and organized is intimately related to your well-being and how you approach life. You can create a living environment that is healthy for your needs. I need you to know that it's possible to unlock your haven.

Promise me that you won't get overwhelmed in this section! Well, just do your best to control the emotion because you'll be doing some deep diving or analyzing that is necessary for the process. This portion of your process is an assessment that will expedite your organizational journey. You want to be clear and the way to be clear is to create a plan regardless of how much or how little you feel needs to be done. You want a well-defined plan. Your plan is not like Suzy's plan. Your plan is not like Nicole's plan. It's not like Keisha's plan either unless one of those are your names. What I'm saying is that your plan is individualized and tailored to what you are aiming to achieve. Identify your specific needs and expectations.

Becoming overwhelmed is a real thing for many people. Conducting a self-assessment and using the charted information collected will allow you to identify your strengths, weaknesses, and areas that you want to improve.

First, choose one area in your home. Carefully look around and **assess your area.** Ask yourself the following questions:

- **How does it feel?**

- **Are my items neatly arranged with plenty of empty space around them? Is this area being used the way that I desire?** *Is there space for you to eat at that dining room table? Do you have space on tables for your electronic laptop/tablet, books, and glass to have a drink? If so, maybe you feel pleased and satisfied with how you've arranged the items.*

- **Am I able to move around freely in a safe manner?**

- **Am I pleased with the decor (e.g., art on the wall, furniture)?**

- **Am I pleased with how I have stored my belongings?**

- **What feelings do I experience when I sit in this area?**

- **Do I feel a sense of tranquility and relaxation?**

- **Am I uncomfortable?**

- **Am I anxious to leave this particular room?**

- **What do I like about this room?**

- **What would I change?**

Your viewpoint matters. I want you to contemplate if you'd like to alter any specific areas in each room. If you have too many knick knacks or pictures arranged on an end table, it might appear over-loaded or even too messy for you.

As you continue to assess, finish the following sentence: **"Regarding the furniture and arrangement of my personal items in this space, it would make me feel better if _____."**

- Maybe you'd like to remove some furniture because over the years you've squeezed in too many pieces or pieces that no longer match who you are as a person at this point in your life.

- If you placed more than one or two wall hangings on each wall of a room, the room might appear cramped or "busy," preventing you from feeling at peace in the room. *Maybe your art or mirror is hung too high or too low and this is bothering you. Maybe not. Maybe there are too many throws or pillows on the sofa or maybe not. Maybe you don't think they're cute anymore or maybe you do.* This is your assessment because this is your space. You know what you like and desire, not Suzy or Nicole unless of course you are Suzie or Nicole.

- When conducting your assessment, focus on how you feel in the room and what would make you feel better. For example, you've always disliked the challenges when entering your spare bedroom because you're now using it as a "catch all" room for all the items you don't know what to do with. Maybe you do know what to do with the items, but you had company coming over and you had to rush to put "stuff" somewhere so you dropped it in this particular room. This room probably makes you feel disgusted and/or overwhelmed as soon as you enter. At this point, there may be a lot of sorting to do to accomplish a better feeling when you enter the room.

In fact, the room could be quite cluttered – stacked up with clothing that doesn't fit.

- Your items may be outdated.

- You may have countless bags and boxes of miscellaneous possessions you never use.

- You may be disappointed in yourself and see the room as a true misuse of the space. You might be thinking, "Why haven't I gotten this room under better control so I can use it as my home office, a space for content creation, an exercise room or maybe a meditation area?"

Gain Clarity

- Gain clarity about how you can best free your home of clutter. A pleasing result will be greater feelings of peace, comfort, and freedom within you.

- Gain clarity on how your space can be more aesthetically pleasing.

Embrace

- Embrace the idea of getting rid of unused and worn out items. Open your mind to the possibilities of what your home will be like whenever you discard unneeded items. *This doesn't mean that you have to get rid of all of your stuff. You may need to make adjustments to obtain a desired look or feeling.* You'll have more room for things you enjoy when you declutter. You'll experience a sense of relief and innovation. This is when you open up space for possibility. The possibilities are endless when you have the items that you need to function at hand.

Imagine

- Imagine everything being at your fingertips. Imagine the time you'll have for goals that you want to accomplish outside of having to clean and organize. You'll have more time to socialize, read, date, travel, start a business or write a book.

I know some of you were thinking that I do these things already. That's wonderful if you're socializing, reading for pleasure or traveling. It's what you want because "it", whatever "it" is, IS POSSIBLE. I just want you to imagine a more simplified life so you don't have to worry about always cleaning and always getting organized. You can have the life that you desire and come home to a functional and aesthetically pleasing space.

HELPFUL HINT:

An organized space can be achieved by you and designed specifically for you. This will grant you more time to live the life that you desire. You can feel peace knowing that the space you are sitting or standing in, is functional and pleasing to you.

- A side benefit of decluttering and/or assembling your space the way you want is how content you'll feel that items not currently being used might be appreciated by someone else. Box items and clothing to drop off at the Salvation Army, Goodwill, or other charitable organizations. **Before the holidays, I like to go through my closet and pull out things with tags (some I can fit and some I can't). I take these items that I haven't worn and put them in gift bags. I just went shopping for others in my own closet. Experience the positive feelings of giving to others. It's a great feeling on so many levels. People who I wouldn't normally give gifts to are now receiving random acts of kindness.**

- Allow yourself to daydream about what it will be like when that space is clear of clutter. Imagine how you'll sleep better. Think about how it'll be easier to clean now that there's less "stuff" around that particular area. You'll experience deeper sleep due to decreased dust lingering in the room. When you wake up and open your eyes, you'll thank yourself. You'll notice your space becoming what you desire.

Maybe you have clutter, maybe it's a lot of clutter or maybe you have minimal to no clutter at all. Taking a good look in each room will help open your eyes to the details in your space. Do that assessment and think about changes you want to make. Ask yourself what would make you smile as it relates to your surroundings.

Be excited. Get excited about ridding yourself of the unnecessary. Daydream about the results you want while you bring that dream to a reality, one room at a time. If you declutter your home, you'll give yourself the precious gift of an uncluttered life.

HELPFUL HINT:

This is your journey. Do not compare your
situation to anyone else's.

Please don't feel like you have to assess each room in one day. Take your time. You may assess one room one day and go to another room every couple of days until each room has been assessed. Remember that this is a process. This is your journey. With that being said, think about where you would like to begin your first assessment.

"*Every time you state what you want or believe, you're the first to hear it. It's a message to both you and others about what you think is possible. Don't put a ceiling on yourself.*"

—Oprah Winfrey

ROOM ASSESSMENT

Use the following section to assess your rooms. For each room, you have a page to diagram, creating a visual representation and a page to write notes for each area being assessed.

Bedroom

Closet

Kitchen

Notes

"What's the world for if you can't make it up the way you want it?"

—Toni Morrison

CHAPTER 5

Your Coach Is Here

I am absolutely thrilled to welcome you to this exciting chapter! I proudly wear two hats that I'm incredibly passionate about – not only am I a certified teacher, but I'm also here as your dedicated coach. So, envision this: I'm not just here to transfer knowledge; I'm here to be your biggest cheerleader, guiding you through every twist and turn of your unique path. Let me tell you that the previous chapters have been preparing you for this moment.

As both an educator, coach, and entrepreneur, my mission has consistently been to illuminate the path of learning, making even the most complex concepts a bit more digestible for you. I am genuinely invested in your personal growth and success.

Please understand, I'm not here solely to drop some organizational tips; I'm here to be more – your ally, your sounding board, and your go-to supporter. Together, let's not just tackle the organizational aspects, but let's embark on a journey where we navigate the intricacies to clear your way to enhance your lifestyle. Your success is my success, and I'm here to ensure we celebrate every milestone along the way. So, let's go!

I'm Ready and You're Ready

If you're anything like me, you're probably wishing for a few extra hours in the day. I mean, we're all given the same 24 hours, but wouldn't it be nice if we could stretch it to thirty? The clock is always ticking. Mornings can be a real struggle when you have to navigate through clutter, sift through items, figure out what is clean or what can fit. You might even need to take a couple of deep breaths and pause to make sure you've gathered everything you need to have a productive day. Some of us go through this routine not just for ourselves but for our kids or spouse. Staring at a bunch of things, sifting through piles and trying to decide what's essential and what's not, can be extremely overwhelming.

If you're like most of us, at some point you have likely come to the conclusion that your life is too cluttered. You have too much to do and aren't able to handle your schedule optimally. You probably own too much stuff and maybe you keep adding more each day. Maybe you just feel confined.

- You may feel like a stranger in your own home.

- Maybe you've inherited a bunch of stuff from family members who are no longer with you.

- Maybe you've got a sentimental streak and hold onto a lot of those precious memories and the stuff that goes along with the memories.

- You may feel like you can tackle this and you can.

It's time. Most people could use some form of decluttering, right? But you may be wondering where to begin when you're buried under piles of clutter, commitments, personal files, and a digital avalanche? Don't worry; I got you, your coach is here to assist.

You are preparing. You are prepared. In your recent readings, you've already delved into knowing the impact of clutter, become even more self-aware, tackled exercises to uncover your desires, assessed your space(s), acquired resources, and gathered insights on simplifying. I'm here to keep pouring into your pool of knowledge. So, let's get to it!

Helpful Tip: Be mindful that at times you will need to give yourself grace. Remind yourself that this is your journey.

Planning to Thrive

There are essential requirements and non-essential elements to consider. A positive mindset is crucial, along with the awareness that achieving organization is attainable. Repeat after me: **My goals are an achievable reality**. One more time: **My goals are an achievable reality.** With that being said, let's lay down what we must remember to do.

- **Set achievable goals.** As easy as this sounds, it's that easy. We make plans to travel, attend weddings, birthday parties, and other celebrations. Getting organized is a huge commitment and we have to make a plan for organizational goals. Whether you are trying to remove years of clutter or just want things in your space to be more aesthetically pleasing, YOU NEED A PLAN. Be clear on your goals so you can execute accordingly. This is why a self-assessment is key.

- **Start small.** If there are many aspects of your life that you're trying to get organized, start with the small pieces first. Avoid getting overwhelmed by the task of organizing. Vow to organize just one room at a time. It doesn't even have to be the entire room at the same time. For instance, in your bedroom, you might want to start with your night stand. You may start with one closet versus two if you have multiple closets in your room. *This is what I recommend when I'm conducting my 1:1 sessions with clients.*

- **Use assessments prior to organizing.** Refer to the rooms that you chose to conduct your assessments. You may have assessed your bathroom, bedroom closet, bedroom, living room or home office. There was even space for you to assess another room that wasn't mentioned. If you have not conducted those assessments, go back and do those exercises because that will guide your decision on where you should begin.

- **Make your selection.** You don't have to organize an entire room at one time. You can start with a desk, a corner, or 1 or 2 book shelves that you find particularly troublesome. Try starting in your bathroom, or better yet, just start by going through the cabinet underneath your bathroom sink. Afterward, you can call it a day and then work on another small project another time. It's nice to start small sometimes because you can see the results in that small space and know that the methods that we have been learning about can be applied in other areas.

- **Go at your own pace.** Take it room by room, throughout your house. When you focus on everything as a whole, it can seem like a lost cause. You'll be surprised how much better you'll feel if you begin to organize in small ways. *Every little bit counts when you're trying to create an organized space. A little bit DOES go a long way when getting organized.*

> **HELPFUL HINT:**
>
> Just remember to pace yourself. You don't have to do
> everything all at once. Just take care of one thing at a time and
> you'll notice the progress.

Materials

This is what you need. As you gear up to tackle your organizational project, the initial impulse often leans towards stocking up on plastic containers, hangers, and other storage boxes. However, this approach can inadvertently exacerbate the issue rather than solve it. Instead of addressing the challenge of where to store your belongings effectively, you may end up merely providing additional spaces for items you don't actually need.

Many of my clients have found themselves surprised after sessions, confronted with a surplus of empty bins and other storage products they believed would alleviate their organizational woes but only ended up complicating matters further.

Anyone who has worked with me knows that I suggest that you pause before acquiring more containers to accommodate items you neither need nor use. People often decide it's time to get organized and, well, sometimes they embark on a shopping spree for items that may not exactly be essential. Sure, there might be a few things that are genuinely needed, but the key here is precision.

Pro Tip: The goal isn't to add more things to our homes that we'll later need to find a place for. To keep things streamlined and respect our time, you want to take the time to sort through your belongings before you go out, adding to a collection of organizational tools that you may not even need to organize your lovely possessions.

I suggest that you begin with 3 bags or boxes. It's what you prefer. If you have heavy-duty garbage bags, use those, but if you have kitchen bags, use those. You can use a marker or pen to write on masking tape to distinguish the bags or boxes.

- 1 Bag or Box is for garbage.

- 1 Bag or Box is for donations.

- 1 Bag or Box is for other items.

The last thing that I want you to do is get caught up in what to use to get started. Don't let anything become a barrier to you getting started with your journey of sorting, rehoming, or "farming" your items.

You may need your phone to set a timer. If you can turn your ringer off, that would be great, but I totally understand if you can't. Just be aware that you want to limit distractions. This is your self-care time. This time is designated to your future, a future of possibilities, structure and ORGANIZATION! Let us begin because you are about to SIMPLIFY, RELEASE and MAINTAIN.

"The quality, not the longevity, of one's life is what is important."
—Dr. Martin Luther King, Jr.

CHAPTER 6

Get Started

Say, "I AM READY for this life and I am ready for more out of life!" I know you are ready for this transformative process of organizing. I can feel it because you are here, you are reading this right now. You made it to this chapter. So, let's begin with this. What I'm about to share with you can be employed in any area that you select. With that being said, choose your area – perhaps it's the TV room. You know, that space where you unwind, binge-watch your favorite shows, and gather with loved ones. It's a room that often accumulates a mix of essentials and knick-knacks. So, why not bring a touch of order to it?

Before you jump in, remember the tip – start small. If it's the TV room, zoom in on the focal point: the thing your TV sits on, complete with storage.

Now, let's get started. Choose a room, a closet, a shelf – wherever you've decided needs a bit of an organizational shift – and let's roll up our sleeves.

Equip yourself with the materials we discussed in Chapter 5. You know the materials that were discussed – garbage bags/boxes, donation bags/boxes, and the oh-so-handy bags/boxes for items that don't quite belong in this space. These are your organizational buddies, so make sure they're handy.

Here's a gentle reminder: Let's begin with three bags or boxes. Why three? Well, we're tackling this with a systematic approach – one for things to keep, one for donations, and one for items that need to be tossed (trash). Don't forget to distinguish the bags or boxes. Label or color-code them; whatever makes the most sense to you.

FIRST: Select an Area

Now, let the decluttering BEGIN. You decide where you want to begin. Take a moment to assess your chosen area and visualize the transformation. So, whether it's the TV room, a closet, or a shelf, the steps remain the same. Begin with a clear vision, armed with your organizational tools. You'll see how your chaos can transform into order. Most importantly, enjoy the process.

HELPFUL TIP:

Work on one room at a time. Rather than becoming overwhelmed with feelings about how much you have to do, commit to declutter your home over the long haul. Do something each day to work toward this goal.

SECOND: Remove Everything

Remove all. This may seem like a lot, but this is how you uncover everything in the area that you are planning to organize. You want to sort through everything in the area that you have chosen so it all has to be visible. That means that the space has to be cleared. As you clear the area, you will find out everything that is there.

After discovering the space you have selected, it's crucial to set the stage by effectively relocating items from the space you're about to transform. Find a designated area with ample room to sort through the belongings you're clearing. This initial step lays the foundation.

HELPFUL TIP:

I always advise my clients to be realistic about the time and energy they allocate to this crucial step. You're my client so I want to advise you to clear and declutter the space promptly, minimizing the risk of overwhelming yourself.

Running out of time midway through the process is a pitfall to avoid at all costs. Leaving your home in a state worse than when you started can be not only annoying, but also counterproductive. By strategically moving items to a designated sorting area, you ensure that the decluttering process remains manageable, allowing for a more effective and satisfying transformation of your space. Keep in mind that the relocation area can be in the same room.

Let me provide you with some examples:

Closet Removal: When organizing your closet, you will be taking everything out of the closet. You can put everything on the bed. The idea here is to create a clean slate, a blank canvas. As you remove your items, you are also evaluating what's in there.

I've found that relocating items to another room during this process can be quite cumbersome. Instead, if space permits, I prefer to lay everything out in the room where I'm working. As each piece comes out of the closet, it's like you're conducting a mini-evaluation, and it's during this recognition that things become apparent.

- Some items might be screaming "out of style!"

- Some items may reveal signs of wear and even tear, like holes or stretched necks.

- You may just say, "I don't want this anymore."

- You may have forgotten that you have owned certain pieces.

This is when the physical shift occurs. With this newfound awareness, you start contemplating the positioning of things. The emphasis here is on intentionality. It's not just about returning items to the closet; it's about curating a collection that aligns with your current style and needs.

So, for now, everything is coming out. The closet is getting stripped down to its bare bones, making room for a thoughtful and purposeful reassembly. It's a process of rediscovery, letting go of the old to make space for the new and ensuring that what goes back in is not just clothes, but a reflection of who you are now and how you want to present yourself to the world with the items that you elect to keep.

Kitchen Removal: One of the most essential rooms in your home is the kitchen. It's a space often begging for an update. Logically speaking, I understand why there would be a strong desire for functionality in this room. So, you may have decided to work in your kitchen. Hold on, it's important to acknowledge all of those details.

- Cabinets: upper and lower

- Drawers

- Countertop/Sink Area

- Refrigerator

- Pantry

- Table/Island

With various nooks and crannies, the kitchen can indeed be a lot. Fear not, because coach Sylvia is here to break it down into manageable portions to avoid feeling swamped.

Step one: Take a deep breath. If this is your starting point or your next area that you have selected, very good! This is an excellent area to organize. Perhaps it's one cabinet or one drawer. Remember that the key is to start small to decrease overwhelm. The process, the steps, remain consistent whether you're organizing a drawer, a shelf, or an entire room.

Let's say you're tackling a cabinet. Utilize your counter space – it's like your organizing canvas. Clear it off and create that clean slate. Remove all the items from the chosen cabinet and lay them out on the counter. If counter space is at a premium, no worries; your kitchen table can serve the same purpose. If neither the counter nor the kitchen table is available, grab those trusty boxes and bags we discussed earlier. They're like little organization helpers, ready to contain the items you're removing, keeping them in check and preventing chaos.

So, whether it's a cabinet, a drawer, or another kitchen nook, the process is about creating order from the ground up. Each step, each item removed, brings you closer to a kitchen that not only looks organized, but functions in a way that's just for you. Embrace the journey, one item or room at a time, and watch as things get transformed in a way that aligns with your vision, path, and lifestyle.

Book Shelf Removal: So, let's say you've made the decision to tackle the organization of a room, be it your office, living room, or any space with some type of shelves. As I've emphasized before, the key is not to overwhelm yourself by trying to conquer too much at one time. Even though the entire room might be on your organizational list, you may have wisely (pat yourself on the back) chosen to start with a bookshelf.

Now, bookshelves can be tricky, especially when they're harboring a multitude of items like knick-knacks, books, and whatever else. In such cases, opting to organize one or two shelves at a time can be a serious game-changer. It's definitely a manageable approach that ensures you're not biting off more than you can chew.

The removal process is a critical phase in which you will be doing a complete evacuation. Personally, if I'm organizing my office, I'll either use my floor or desk to hold items. This may be an unrealistic option though. Your desk might be covered with clutter. In that case, you can opt to lay down a sheet on the floor, creating a makeshift staging area for the items. Alternatively, if you've got that handy bag or box we discussed using earlier, toss your items in there. It's a simple yet effective way to keep things contained during the removal process.

There's a good chance you'll stumble upon items you forgot you even had. That's the beauty of this method - it's not just an organizing; it's your path of self-discovery. Don't be afraid to strip those shelves bare, lay everything out, and conduct a thorough assessment.

It's in these moments that you might uncover hidden treasures, make decisions about what to keep or let go, and ultimately transform your shelves into a curated display that tells your new story.

Use What You've Got!

Removing all is necessary. Alright, let's delve a bit deeper into some practical examples of how to go about the removal process. As I mentioned earlier, there's flexibility in where you can temporarily relocate your items during this stage of organization.

The Floor

Utilizing the floor is a fantastic option. Clear a space, lay down a sheet, and boom – you've got an impromptu staging area. It's a straightforward yet effective method, allowing you to see everything at a glance and assess your possessions with ease.

The Bed

Your bed is another fantastic surface to use. Spread out a clean sheet or blanket, and your bed instantly transforms into a makeshift holding ground. This option is particularly beneficial if the area around your shelves is limited or if you're working in a smaller space.

Other Furniture

Don't overlook the potential of other furniture in your home. Coffee tables, dining tables, or even an empty dresser can serve as temporary holding spots. The idea is to create an environment where you can visually and physically engage with each item, ensuring a thorough evaluation.

The key principle here is to begin with a clean slate. Whether it's the floor, your bed, or another piece of furniture, starting with an empty space allows for a fresh perspective. It sets the stage for a deliberate and thoughtful process, ensuring that as you reintroduce items with purpose and intentionality. So, pick your preferred space, and clear it out completely.

Decluttering is a decision. This is a reflection of your lifestyle. When you are sorting and decluttering, you are taking a moment to pick up each item. In that quick moment, I want you to ask yourself three fundamental questions:

1. "Do I use this regularly?"

2. "Do I love this?"

3. "Is this a necessity?"

If the answer to these queries is a resounding "no," it's a sign that the item may have outlived its purpose in your life. It's time to part ways.

We're basically scrutinizing every single thing in our space. If an item has been playing hide-and-seek in the shadows without serving a purpose, it's giving us a not-so-subtle nudge that it's time to part ways.

Now, let's talk about those items that have seen better days – you know, the soiled, broken, stained, or worn-out items. It's decision time. Tossing them into the great beyond might just be the most logical move. And for the ones that are beyond the rescue mission, well, they're making a one-way trip to the trash.

My mother watches antique shows where the expert evaluates the condition of an item and its value. You're kind of like that expert right now. No, you are the expert because these are your belongings, you have all the background knowledge and the control. Think of yourself as a decluttering expert where every item gets a fair evaluation. If it's not contributing to the positive vibes and functionality of your space, it's time for it to find a new purpose elsewhere. So, let's simplify. Make some tough calls, bid farewell to the non-contributors, and create a space that is organized and will allow you to thrive. It's your decluttering show, and each item has its role to play in the narrative of a more organized and refreshed environment. Let the purging begin or continue!

HELPFUL TIP:

Imagine you're on one of those antique shows my mom loves, and you're the expert, sizing up each item – but in this case, it's your own stuff.

Remember, decluttering is not merely about creating physical space; it's a conscious decision-making process that shapes your environment and, by extension, your lifestyle. The more you let go, the less cluttered your space will feel, granting you the freedom to curate a living space that truly resonates with you.

Whether you're gaining newfound space or investing extra time in housing items, each decision is a step forward. You're not just decluttering; you're taking control of your space and, in turn, your life. This is a journey of awareness, where you become intimately acquainted with every item you own. Bit by bit, as you declutter your space, you're making progress – progress that aligns with your intentions and propels you towards a more intentional and organized life.

Pro Tip: Get rid of items that you no longer use. Think and act on organizing things you really want to keep and most importantly, the things that you need to keep. *Your mental health is worth preserving.*

THIRD: Sort and Categorize

Let's break down the what and why of sorting and classifying because, trust me, it's not just about putting things in neat little piles.

- Sorting: When we talk about sorting, we mean grouping items based on certain characteristics like color, shape, size – you get the idea.

- Classifying: Now, classifying takes it up a notch by applying a characteristic to a group (think all circles together, all the big stuff in its own league).

Well, sorting and classifying are like the dynamic duo. They help us notice the details of how things are alike and different. Think about how children explore objects, they're not just playing; they're learning about attributes and relationships. Like, "Hey, these blocks are all big, so let's give them their own space. And these toys? Oh, these are all circles – let's get them together."

But here's the magic – sorting and classifying introduce children to pattern recognition, and set the foundation for higher-level math and science. Sorting and classifying is also the groundwork that we need for our journey. Let's go!

Taking control of your space begins with sorting through your items, and let me tell you, it's a must-do. The same items that were once scattered, creating chaos, now need your attention because when you get this done, you open up for new possibilities. It's time to bring order through categorizing.

Think about grouping similar items together. It's the key to creating a system that not only looks organized, but is. Once sorted, you're going to find a place for that group of items. Those items will need a home, and the way you sort or categorize them plays a serious role in you gaining access to those items.

Bedroom Closet. Imagine you're standing in front of your bedroom closet, ready to get them in an order that's suitable for your lifestyle, your set-up. Those clothes that you took out of your closet that may be on your bed need to be sorted so it's time to think about categories.

- If you're a business professional or attend church, gather all your suits together. That's a category. A category is a family of items that belong together.

- Long dresses? Yep, they get their own category too.

- Denim is a category.

- Formal is a category.

- You can sort by type, grouping all the button-down shirts together.

- If you're like me, sort by color. It's your system, it's what you desire.

Sorting is one of my favorite things to do and is also a crucial step in organization. Sorting is like the architect's blueprint for your organizational masterpiece. It's not just about putting things in their place; it's a methodical categorization. It's a meticulous process, but in a good way because it is only going to make you great. Just keep visualizing the end goal.

TV Room. Imagine you've chosen the TV room. The TV stand, with its mix of remotes, DVDs (probably not, but maybe some are lingering), and who knows what else, is calling for attention.

1. First, gather your materials – those trusty bags and boxes we've discussed before. You need them. Each bag has a distinct purpose, so don't forget to label them.

2. Remove everything in the space you're working.

3. Begin sorting. Look at each item on the TV stand and decide its fate.

   - Is it a keeper?

   - Does it need to be donated?

   - Is its time up? Is it destined for the trash?

> **HELPFUL HINT:**
>
> Channel your organized self and group similar items together
> – remotes with remotes. Group your items.

- Sorting is more than just physically shifting items around; it's a mental workout, an opportunity to reevaluate the significance and role of each possession. Think of it as being therapeutic because in this process, you might stumble upon some revelations.

- You may discover that you have bought way too much of something. Let's say that you find five candles on a shelf. You may say to yourself, "Do I really need all five?" Probably not. Maybe you'll decide to light one immediately, while you continue to sort. You might bag one up as a thoughtful gift for a friend who has a birthday approaching. You may trash a candle that is very low on wax.

Alright, let's cut to the chase here. We're in full-on declutter mode, and it's your call on how you want to roll with it. Personally, I'm not into hanging on to a bunch of candles with just a smidge of wax left when I can easily switch to a heat warmer. Maybe down the road, I'll reconsider, but for now, it's all about shedding the excess.

So, if we're talking declutter mode, let's be real about it – those candles with barely a hint of wax left? They're hitting the trash. It's about creating a space that resonates with the vibe you want, and right now, it's the minimalist, clutter-free scene that's calling my name.

Now, this is your journey, so do what feels right for you. Just remember, it's not just about cleaning up; it's about adopting a lifestyle that suits you. Choose what vibes with your space, trash those candles or keep them – the power is in your hands. This is your world; let's make it one you're happy to live in.

As you sift and sort through your stuff, you might find yourself rearranging not just items, but also your priorities. That surplus of candles could prompt you to think – am I still as into candles as I once was? Perhaps not, and that's okay. In this moment, the option to donate those candles might become a meaningful choice.

Your decisions matter. Things will begin to transform because of your intentional choices. Those random items that once cluttered the space will now be part of a system that makes sense to you.

Sorting, at its core, is a mindful journey. It's about making intentional decisions, understanding the value each and every item brings. You want to make space for what truly matters. So, whether it's candles, books, pencils or pens, let each decision be a step toward a more purposeful space.

Whether you're sorting the TV room, a closet, or a shelf, remember the power of categorization. It's your guide to a space that not only looks organized, but resonates with your unique style and needs.

Pro Tip: Consider grouping items that you typically need or use at the same time.

Have fun with sorting and really embrace the process and remember that this is your path. It's not just about putting things back in their place; it's about curating a system that reflects your lifestyle and makes your items easily accessible when you need them. Sorting is your secret weapon in transforming chaos into order, one category at a time. This is how you'll thrive.

Now that you've conquered the sorting and categorizing phase, take a moment to enjoy your newfound space – give yourself a pat on the back! Seriously, major kudos for making it to this point; I know it can be a bit of a grind, but the good thing is that – it's so worth it because knowing what you own is a game-changer. It's like having a detailed map of your possessions. Not to mention, the satisfaction of having everything grouped together in these neat little cities or towns, thanks to your hard work.

Now comes the exciting part – it's all exciting to me. It's time to give each item a home, a designated spot where it can live its best organized life. Think of it as assigning addresses to your belongings. It's the next step in the organizational saga, and trust me, the rewards just keep on coming. So, gear up for the assignment phase; your possessions are about to get some prime real estate in your newly organized space. Let the home assignments begin!

Fourth: Assignments, Please...

Once again, your decision matters. Here we are, once again, at the crossroads of decision-making because, guess what, these items need a home. After the sorting and categorizing phase, this is the moment of truth. What's cool is, these items might not find their way back to the original spot they occupied before this whole process kicked off. It's like you get a chance for everything to have a fresh start – some might go back to their old spot, while others may be getting relocated.

The beauty of it all lies in how you want to access your items. It's your space, and your call. Each item, big or small, deserves its own VIP spot – a designated space that is easy for you to locate and access. This isn't a cookie-cutter operation; oh no, we're customizing this living situation for each and every possession. So, let the organizational bliss unfold, and create a space that caters to your unique style and needs.

Now, it's like you're sending each item off to its personal homeroom. Picture it as a little adventure – the item just graduated from 8th grade, is now in highschool, off it goes to its new homeroom, and you're the principal behind the relocation.

Whether it's your favorite pen, shea butter, a vase, a picture frame, flat irons or that quirky decorative piece, wherever you decide to place it becomes its official home. And please, please– remember it's all about accessibility. I know I keep saying that, but that's only going to help you with an all-star lifestyle. In your home or office, this will allow you to win!

You want to know exactly where each item resides. So, think strategically. Imagine where you'd love to find that item when you need it, and boom – that's its new home. Now, off you go, or shall I say, off it goes to its designated spot. This is how the genius of organization happens, one well-thought-out home at a time.

Consider utilizing organizational tools that you already have on hand. Repurpose containers from around your home – it's a savvy move that saves money. If you do need to purchase storage containers, make a detailed list to steer clear of unnecessary splurges and unnecessary clutter.

Fifth: Contain Those Items

Absolutely, we're getting exposed to tricks of professional organizers! Putting your items into containers isn't just for the aesthetic; it's a strategic move, ensuring functionality and easy access. That's what you really need to know because making your daily life smoother and more organized is the goal. Now, I haven't made a big deal about it because, truth be told, I don't want you caught up in a shopping frenzy or a look that might not match how you move, your lifestyle.

The most important part is to follow the steps that have been laid out earlier just for you – knowing your desires, establishing where you want to begin, clearing that area, sorting and categorizing, figuring out where you want things to reside, finding homes for your items – and then, you contain them.

I mention this at this point in our journey because, let's face it, social media can be a bit of an influence and sometimes a distraction. But here's the thing – this process is all about you and your thrive. It's about strategically aligning your space with your lifestyle.

Oh, the tales I could tell! Countless potential clients call me up, all excited, saying, "Sylvia, I've got the bins, I've got new containers – I'm ready to get you in here to start the organization!" In my head, though, it's like a silent scream, a resounding "NOOOOOOOOOOO!" You see, the key is to kick off the organizing journey before you even think about hitting the stores.

One time, I had a client who was convinced that the solution to her clutter chaos was just a shopping spree away. She was so happy to show off her shiny new bins, baskets, and containers – a bunch of really cool organizational tools. But, and it's a big but, because it wasn't necessary yet. First, we have to thoroughly assess, clear, sort, and categorize. That's when you know what containers you truly need.

So, the moral of this story is: before you go on that shopping spree, back it up a little bit. Trust me; you'll thank yourself later. Your tools could be right under your nose. Start the process and use what you've got! You have things in your home that you really don't use often or may have forgotten even exist. Those are the ones you want to begin using when you contain them. It might take a bit of creative thinking, but hey, most of those containers may just be within arm's reach. Also, after organizing, you may have found some things that you forgot about so no need to hit the stores just yet.

You might have this crystal-clear vision of your dream look, and guess what? It might not be within the four walls of your current space. No rush, no pressure, just give it a bit of time to percolate. Now, if you're dead-set on a particular aesthetic, and you're certain it's not vibing with your current setup, go for it! Treat yourself to what you envision; you've earned it!

HELPFUL HINT:

Things get uncovered when you're organizing so don't be so quick to go shopping for organizational tools that may be uncovered after organizing an entire room, two or even three.

Here's a list of things that people often have, want, or desire for their organized homes. Feel free to use it at your leisure, no rush. Let the organizational shift continue! Let's be savvy about the tools we use to contain. Space is provided in case you think of an area you can place this or jot any other notes or ideas.

- **Door Organizers:** Unlock a whole new world of organization and efficiency with the backs of closet doors. That's one of the most underused storage spots in the home. You can put yours to work by organizing your gift-wrapping supplies, craft materials or bottles/jars in the pantry.

- **Storage Bins and Baskets**: Versatile and cost-effective, these are perfect for grouping similar items such as picture albums, toys, games, books, movies, TV equipment, throw blankets, and so much more. You can stash the baskets underneath a console table, so they're out of the way, but easy to reach when needed.

- **Drawer Organizers**: Where do you have drawers? Drawer organizers are versatile and ideal for separating and categorizing in the kitchen, office, bedroom or anywhere you see drawers. Things like kitchen utensils, socks, or office supplies can safely and neatly be placed out of sight. Drawer dividers customize your drawers for various items, ensuring a clutter-free space. With these organizers, you can easily find what you need without rummaging through a cluttered drawer.

Think about where these items can live in your world. Remember that people often have these items. Don't feel pressured to buy these because you see it listed. In your notes, you may write the following:

- I could do this in my pantry.

- I definitely don't need this.

- I'd like to get a new version.

- I no longer need the _____ that I have and my cousin could use this.

- **Shoe Racks:** These can be used to keep shoes off the floor or unconventional ways for storing paper towels, trash bags, other cleaning supplies, and cleaning tools. For years I had a shoe rack installed in my classroom closet and I used it for paper towels, cleaning materials and other things. It became the go-to spot for all of my classroom essentials such as plastic baggies, pencils, crayons and alphabet tiles.

- **Hanging Shelves:** Maximize vertical space in your closets – great for folded clothes or shoes. I used to have one in my college apartment that was excellent for hanging hoodies and logo T-shirts.

- **Under-Bed Storage:** Perfect for seasonal items (e.g. swimwear, hats, scarves, ski attire) Some of my clients use them to store purses, shoes and even documents.

- **Hooks and Pegs:** Utilize wall space for hanging items like bags, hats, or accessories (e.g. earrings, necklaces.

- **Trays:** Ideal for holding a plant, whatever you can imagine on a coffee table, a desk, holding a random pile of magazines or envelopes.

- **Lazy Susan:** These bad boys are like the MVPs in a kitchen, bathroom, pantry etc. Similar to trays, they do an excellent job of keeping items in check, and the best part? Unlike your typical tray, a Lazy Susan comes with a game-changing feature – it can twirl.

- **File Organizers:** For paperwork, bills, or any important documents – keep that paperwork game strong.

- **Clear Containers**: Ideal for anything. Many people use them for shoes, office supplies, pantry items, crafting supplies, or anything you want to see at a glance.

When you give each item its designated home, whether it's a drawer, a bin, or a shelf, you're creating order. It's not just about appearances; it's about making life simpler. Imagine needing a specific item and knowing exactly where to find it. That's the beauty of containment – having a precise place for everything, and everything in that place.

To Contain or Not to Contain, That is the Question

Now, let's go in detail about containers – a little more clarity. Here's the deal: a classy picture frame sitting on a shelf? No container necessary. It's doing its thing, looking all elegant and doesn't need containment.

Now, my twelve bottles of nail polish? Yep, those definitely need a container to keep them from staging a colorful takeover. Same goes for my seven makeup brushes – they get their own cozy container as well.

> **HELPFUL HINT:**
>
> Not everything in your space needs a container.

Let there be no confusion. When you get to this point you have already sorted and categorized your items. Let's just say that some of the items have closed on a home and don't have furniture yet. These items need to be contained. Let's break it down with two columns, because organization is all about strategy.

1. The first list is your game plan – items that need to be contained (these items need a container).

2. The second list – the containment plan, to contain that/those items (what you will use). Think about what containers or tools are stepping up to keep each item in order? It might be a bin or a basket or even a hook.

Please Contain Me

List 1 Needs Containment	List 2 Tool Used to Contain Item

Please Contain Me

List 1 Needs Containment	List 2 Tool Used to Contain Item

Once you've masterfully contained those items – the ones begging for containers and the ones you just love having in containers – it's time to go into a new area. Here's what to do as stated in the steps:

1. **Find an area to tackle.**

2. **Clear it.**

3. **Place the items somewhere that you can comfortably sort and categorize.**

4. **Assign homes to those items based on their categories, ensuring easy access.**

5. **Contain them if need be in your signature style.**

Now, don't stop there. You are going to repeat the process with each space – find another spot, clear, sort and categorize, designate homes, and contain. Again and again. I think you've got it! Keep doing it, repeat the steps, and before you know it, you've created a living situation that's not just accessible, but also perfectly aligned with your needs.

Go a little further each day. Take it one step at a time. Once you've started, keep that momentum going. Tackle one area, conquer it, and then smoothly transition to the next. Now, let's talk about your arch-nemesis – perfection. Trust me, it's not your friend here. This doesn't have to be a quest for perfection; it's about getting started and staying the course with the steps provided.

Your efforts, no matter how small, are stepping stones to progress. So, make it a breeze for yourself. Ease into the process, celebrate the victories, and remember, it's about the journey, not the flawless destination.

Get some help. Listen up, because sometimes we all need a little backup. If you're feeling swamped or overwhelmed by the thought of tackling some tasks or this journey solo, it's time to call in reinforcements. Don't hesitate to reach out to a friend – someone reasonable who's willing to lend a hand. Now, they don't need to be a pro organizer or have their life together – they just need to be there for you, offering grace, patience, and maybe even a gentle push when needed.

I get it, you may be feeling an array of feelings, but trust me and start. The rewards are worth it. With the right support system in place, you'll find yourself making strides towards greatness. So, don't be afraid to ask for help and surround yourself with friends who've got your back. Together, we'll conquer that clutter and revel in the satisfaction of a job well done.

Don't get overwhelmed. Try to make a positive step forward each day even if it's something small. You'll soon find that your life will become more manageable and you'll feel a great deal of satisfaction!

Thrive

LTOY

Part Three
Maintain

"For some it happens sooner than others. For some it looks as if it's not happening at all, but as sure as you maintain and keep faith within your own self, you won't be daunted by appearances, and you won't give up."
-Phylicia Rashad

CHAPTER 7

How to Maintain the Progress

Bravo and congratulations! You've officially entered the maintenance phase, and let me tell you that this marks the beginning of a whole new chapter for you. Consider yourself adorned with a well-deserved badge of victory – you've shown yourself that conquering desires, strategies and/or clutter is not just a dream; it's a tangible reality. Now, it's all about saluting yourself for an environment that you achieved and keeping it all together. Maintaining your progress is important and this can be achieved by establishing routines. With this achievement comes focusing on new desires from here on out. The key is consistency and mindset.

Sure, many of us think of January as the kickoff for your fresh start, but let's be real – every season, and even every month, from here on out is a great opportunity to reassess and purge if needed. This proactive approach ensures you don't become too attached to things that have overstayed their welcome.

Stay on top of your decluttering game, and keep your space in a manner feasible to your liking. You might ask, how do I stay on top of my decluttering game? Well.....

- If that juicer isn't juicing, toss it.

- If that make-up is old, stop playing and get rid of it.

- If that flat iron stopped getting hot, you know what I'm about to say –TOSS IT!

- If you're obsessed with sheets like me, that means you have a few sets or more than a few sets. If you get an undesirable stain on your sheets, you should toss them. Think about it, you can only have one set on your bed at a time.

- If that shredder doesn't work the same, replace it with a new one. Keep it until you get a new one.

- If that glass in that picture frame cracked, stop playing like you are going to replace the glass. I think you know what I'm about to say if you have picked up on this pattern.

- If that donation bag or bin is full, take it to the person or site where you want it to go.

- Set a date each month to drop off items that don't belong in your space.

HELPFUL HINT:

Your house is not a storage facility or a dumping ground.

- If something's broken, it may be time to let it go. Donate it, recycle it, or toss it in the trash—just don't hang onto it if it's not bringing any value to your life.

- If it's too big for you to wear or doesn't look flattering, donate it or give it to a friend.

- If your shoe heel breaks, take them to the shoe shop or trash them.

- If you have unattractive/undesirable throw pillows and you just got some new ones, please don't hold on to the old ones.

After embarking on the journey of decluttering and getting organized, it's so important to make a conscious effort to maintain order. So, uphold the newfound order. Personally, I find that sustaining this order can become second nature, even if occasional slip-ups occur. These slip-ups typically occur during particularly hectic periods, when life gets busier than usual. Thankfully, bouncing back during such phases is a straightforward process. With that being said, let's stay on course. The upcoming segment provides an opportunity to confidently put your best foot forward. Let's get to the plan.

MAKE A PLAN

Break down the ongoing upkeep into manageable action items. Think of these as the refined steps to sustain the current order effortlessly. Since you're already aware of your destination – it's time to curate a list of tasks that will serve as your maintenance routine. These tasks should be easily achievable within short time frames, let's say about 5 to 30 minute spans, allowing you to integrate them into your daily schedule without feeling burdened.

Organize and clean a little bit everyday. Here's a simple yet effective mantra: Do a little bit every day! You may elect to invest ten or twenty minutes daily into organizing your space, and you'll witness a substantial transformation. This small, consistent effort will get you some remarkable results in maintaining a clutter-free environment. By spending just ten or twenty minutes a day organizing your space, you'll be making a huge difference.

> **HELPFUL TIP:**
>
> Break down your chores throughout the week to dodge the overwhelm of a marathon cleaning session.

By staying one step ahead and strategizing your cleaning/maintenance plan, you'll be the master of your domain in no time. You'll find yourself effortlessly in control so grab that favorite pen of yours, and let's put this plan into action.

Trust me, you'll function a whole lot better when you've got a plan in place. Some tasks can be done once a week, while others can be done only once a month. Grab yourself a calendar, and if needed, slap it up on the wall or keep it digital for an easy reference.

1. Take a stroll through each room.

2. Think of what it needs and the frequency of those needs.

3. Under each idea, jot down whether you'll be maintaining that area daily (D), weekly (W), monthly (M), once a year (Y), or maybe something entirely different.

Laundry: Assigning a specific day of the week can help this process. I know that some people wash all of their towels on a particular day and clothes on another day. Think about your approach. What's a good day for you to wash?

Refrigerator: Every week I raid the refrigerator for food that may be expired or rotten. I do this the morning of our garbage day.

Desk: Designate a day(s) to declutter your computer desk – this may take about ten minutes.

Vehicle(s): If you drive, scan your vehicle for the unnecessary and discard.

TV Room: Do a daily sweep of items that don't belong.

Task	D	W	M	Y	NOTES
Laundry					
Refrigerator					
Toiletries					
Linen Closet					
Computer Desk/Area					
Car/Vehicle(s)					
TV Room					
Bathroom(s)					
Microwave					
Air Fryer					
Oven					
Buffet/Island					
Drawers					
Dresser					
Chest					
Closet					
China Cabinet					
Laundry Room					
Basement					
Garage					
Shed					

What else would you add to your calendar? Continue to brainstorm on the lines provided and then add ideas to your calendar.

_____

_____

_____

_____

_____

SCHEDULE TO MAINTAIN

What's important for you so you can feel adequate to freely tackle your long term and short term goals? If spring cleaning for your space was a burden on you, it probably means that you let things get out of hand this year. You can prevent it from happening again by doing periodic cleaning of your space. Make a plan for Monday, Tuesday, Wednesday, Thursday, you get the idea. Don't think that you have to do a whole lot. You are in the maintenance phase. You are in control of your plan so go ahead and MAINTAIN!

It's much more manageable compared to attempting to clean your entire place in one evening! Trust me, you don't want to have a date night, family, or friends visit and you're in a panic because clutter is in the way. Choose a specific day for doing your tasks. You may say that you're going to do laundry, while watching a movie – a perfect time to fold clothes as well. Even tasks we usually dread, like drying and folding clothes, can become more bearable if scheduled wisely. So make that schedule. If you need an extra hand, don't hesitate to delegate tasks to other family members. Team effort makes the entire process a whole lot smoother!

Delegate Tasks: Learning to delegate chores is a crucial skill in maintaining an organized and smooth functioning home, especially with a large family. Hey, it's okay to ask for help. Perhaps your home is too big or too disorganized for you to feel comfortable tackling it on your own. Maybe you're just too busy. Spouses and kids are a great place to start asking for help. After all, they live there, too! They certainly contribute to dirt and clutter. Setting up established routines ensures that specific tasks are completed daily, providing a clear plan for everyone to follow.

Who is Doing What?

- Who is dumping the garbage?

- Who is washing the dishes?

- Who is sweeping the floor? Make it known.

Take the guesswork out of it. Kids always want a little something and guess what? So do you.

Consider assigning responsibilities to each family member to contribute to the organization and upkeep of your home. By giving everyone specific tasks, the expectations are clear. You may have to sit down with your family and have a discussion. Let them know, "We can collectively work towards maintaining a tidy and orderly living space. It not only lightens the load, but also instills a sense of shared responsibility among us."

HELPFUL TIP:

Sometimes you may feel alone in this process. It's okay to ask for help. No one expects you to become super-organized overnight.

Family Fun with Organizing

To make the process more enjoyable, turn it into a game that involves the entire family. Getting rid of things can be contagious. You'll likely find that everyone else in your household will jump on the bandwagon when they see how great your personal space looks. You'll feel a new found freedom each day when you awake. When everyone is involved, tasks are completed more efficiently, and it becomes a collective effort. Plus, it's an excellent way for families to spend quality time together while accomplishing necessary chores. I know that if a family member needs an important document, I know where to get it. Have those discussions. Those conversations become organic when you are cleaning and organizing together.

Depending on your child's age and development, it's not your responsibility to clean your child's room. Make sure they take ownership of their own tasks. Sure, you may have to model it, more than once. Go ahead and delegate chores to your spouse and/or children. Dividing the work among many family members teaches everyone how to work together as a team.

Being an educator and a coach, I completely get that not every child is ready for the same tasks. I'm just saying, allow your children to contribute. The University of Arkansas System created an age appropriate chore chart for children ages 2 to early teenage years.

Below you'll find examples of chores that can help inform your choices when assigning chores to your children:

» **2 to 3-year-olds:** They can start putting toys and groceries away and even try dressing themselves.

» **4 to 5-year-olds:** Involve them in feeding pets, attempting to make their beds (maybe not perfectly, but it's a start), and helping clear the table after dinner.

» **6 to 7-year-olds:** This age group can handle wiping tables and counters, putting away laundry, and trying to sweep floors.

» **7 to 9-year-olds:** They can level up to loading and unloading the dishwasher, assisting with meal prep, and packing their own lunch for school.

» **10 to 11-year-olds:** Give them tasks like changing their sheets, taking charge of kitchen or bathroom cleaning, and even contributing to yard work.

» **12 and above:** They're ready for more responsibility, such as washing the car and assisting with younger siblings. Teens can step up with grocery shopping and running errands.

Acknowledge and respect each child's individual strengths and readiness when assigning tasks. These are suggestions and it is essential to consider each child's unique capabilities and readiness for different tasks.

- Tell your family members, "Let's work together to make our home a more organized and pleasant place for everyone."

- When they are on board or complete a task, let them know that you appreciate their cooperation and involvement in maintaining a functional environment for the family.

- When they show willingness or finish a task, express your gratitude in your own way for their contribution.

Kids pick up a ton of valuable lessons from tackling household chores. When they do chores, they're not just learning to handle responsibilities – they're gearing up with life skills that'll serve them well when they hit adulthood. Think beyond just organizing; we're talking cooking, cleaning, even a bit of gardening. Exposure is always important. Taking all the weight off adults also helps.

Organizing is teamwork and relationship-building. Clear communication, cooperation, and working as a team can become second nature. Plus, there's a confidence boost in it for the little ones, just like us grown-ups. Even if they're not exactly thrilled about the task at hand, it will give them that sweet satisfaction of a job well done when it's done.

Here's the real tea: Sharing the load of housework isn't just about clean spaces. It's about combating family stress. When everyone does their part, things run smoother, and the whole family comes out on top. So, let those kids do some chores – it's not just about getting things done; it's about building skills and making family life a little less chaotic. You may consider setting up a chore system.

Here's a simple chore plan:

- **Family Meeting**: Start by holding a family meeting to discuss recent organizational challenges and establish goals for family chores. Share your expectations and make sure your child or partner understands what's expected for each chore. by being clear.

- **Create a Chore List**: Share a list of chores you expect to be completed, including special or less frequent tasks. Clearly communicate the expectation of each chore to be done to avoid confusion. Ask for suggestions. For example, when cleaning a room, clarify what "clean" means for that expectation – is everything in its place, are dirty clothes in a hamper, is the bed made?

- **Chore Chart:** You can create or buy a chore chart and incorporate an incentive plan. Ensure there are more opportunities to earn chore points. Make the point system enticing, allowing them to earn points for activities or items they desire. Give reminders during the first week to help them get accustomed to the plan. Maybe your child wants to have company over or to buy a new game. Those are the incentives.

- **Family Incentive:** Discuss a family incentive, choosing one that matches your family's preferences. Decide on a point value for this incentive, keeping it reasonable and attainable. Maybe you all can go out for ice cream, to the movies or out for pizza.

Feel free to keep it simple when tracking chores. Use stickers, points, tallies, or initials—whatever works best for you and your child. The key is to establish a chore system that promotes teamwork and helps your child grasp the significance of responsibilities and positive behavior. Keeping it straightforward ensures everyone stays on the same page and enjoys the process.

Organizing is definitely a skill that might take some time to learn. While it might seem quicker to handle chores by yourself, guiding your child through the process will pay off in the long run. If you find yourself revisiting a task to ensure it's done correctly, it's likely just part of the learning curve. Choosing a chore that suits your child's abilities will boost the chances of success. Start small and remember, it's all about setting them up for success while they develop their organizational skills.

Treat Yourself: Life is this incredible time and we know time, it sure does zip by, often catching us off guard. I'm not saying that to be a downer; it's just a little nudge to soak up every ounce of joy from the time we've got. When you find yourself thinking, "Where did the time go?" take a moment, gather yourself, and remind yourself to savor every single beat of the clock.

This concept is relevant to organization. It's a gentle push to treat yourself, to indulge in things that make every moment feel like it's worth it. One of those indulgences could very well be bringing in – a professional cleaning service.

If you've got the financial means, don't hesitate to treat yourself to a professional cleaning once a month or every few months—it's like giving yourself a really nice gift. The impact is truly something else when your space is not just clean, but also well-organized. Let me emphasize, well-organized. Having order in place makes it much easier for those cleaning pros to navigate your systems. While the occasional professional cleaning is a great boost, remember, your cleaning and organizing calendar is the main piece in keeping you on track. So, let's not forget the power of a well-planned schedule to maintain that tip-top order that's going to make you feel good.

Storage: Plan a strategy to store similar things together in marked storage bins. Make good use of shelves, baskets, or furniture with built-in storage space to keep things neat and where you're likely to need them. Investing in practical storage containers can truly transform your life. Now is the perfect time to purchase storage solutions. I didn't want to stress this until the maintenance stage. Why? Because you've already sorted through all your belongings and identified what you need to keep. With a clear understanding of your storage needs and approximate sizes required, you can make more accurate purchases, saving you time and hassle of returning unnecessary items.

Additionally, you'll find that some storage boxes and accessories not only serve a functional purpose, but also add a decorative touch to your living space, complementing your existing decor.

- Consider placing a storage container conveniently in your closet. As you come across items you no longer use or wear, simply toss them into the box. Before you know it, your closet will undergo a refreshing cleanup, effortlessly creating space and decluttering your wardrobe.

- For organizing cleaning products or toiletries, caddies can be a convenient solution, while adhesive hooks are perfect for hanging items without the need for nails, preserving your walls.

- Jewelry trays are excellent for separating and organizing your accessories, ensuring they remain easily accessible yet neatly arranged.

- Space bags for storing seasonal items efficiently, maximizing your storage space while keeping your belongings safe and protected.

HELPFUL TIP:

By incorporating these practical storage solutions into your home, you'll be able declutter effortlessly, making your living space more functional and visually appealing.

PREVENT A PILE UP: Incorporate a quick daily purge into your routine to clear away the stuff accumulating on your desk or kitchen counters. Not only will this open up more space, but it'll also provide a clearer picture of what's happening overall.

Toss out any junk immediately and file away those crucial papers. The longer they linger in a pile, the higher the chances of them vanishing into the abyss of forgetfulness.

Now, let's talk about habits. Small changes can make life a whole lot easier. Take those dirty dishes, for instance. Instead of letting them pile up for days, set a designated time at the end of each day or in the mornings to wash them. It might only take a few minutes, and you'll save yourself the hassle of dealing with a towering mountain of dishes. Time-saving and sanity-preserving—now, that's a win-win!

Another way to create a pile up is thinking you're going to do something and never doing it. I'm a huge fan of HGTV, just like millions of others. But let's be real – not everything is a DIY moment. Sure, you can tackle some fixes to save a few bucks, but let's have an honest conversation with ourselves. Ask, "Am I genuinely going to fix this? Will I follow through to keep it in a condition that elevates my space and pleases the eye?" Consider your time and resources. Is this a task that you can realistically handle, or is it something worth delegating? If that's the case, then handle your business and please send me pictures.

Sort Your Mail

Daily mail and papers are the biggest clutter culprit. Stay on top of documents you don't need that might contain personal information. I could easily suggest handling your bills pronto to dodge future worries, but hey, I get it—I don't know the ins and outs of your financial situation. What I do know is that some folks might have the funds and yet procrastinate on bill payments.

My friendly advice: If you've got the means, don't delay—just pay. It's all about keeping that credit score tight or shall I say in top-notch shape. Don't forget about the Sharon Method or the Sylvia Mail Method.

Declutter Your Calendar: Your calendar may need an assessment as well. It is about learning to say "no" to commitments that aren't important to you. Make a list of commitments and put them in order from most important to least important. Keep the top few and remove the rest from your life.

Constantly Get Rid of Clutter

Get rid of your clutter. I can not say this enough. Clutter can creep in our homes in the blink of an eye. Whether it's a bag, samples from a store, business cards, or excess food. We have to control it all.

- Consider living by the rule that if you haven't used an item in over a year and it doesn't hold sentimental value, you should probably consider letting go of it.

- Establish the habit of picking up as you go. When you take something out of its place to use it, put it back when you're done.

- Swap things out. During holidays and other heavy shopping seasons, try discarding at least one item to make room for each new purchase. For example, if you're purchasing a new computer, give your used computer to a local nonprofit.

- Sell unused items. For example, your old bedroom set can be sold on an online platform.

- Remember to donate whenever you can. Donating is a form of recycling. If it's too big or too small, give it to a friend, family member or nonprofit organization.

It may sound redundant, but things will start appearing in your space and once they are there, it's up to you to care for these items. That could mean finding a place for it to live in your space and maybe even having to dust this item. So be cognizant of the fact that you'll have to take care of it.

HELPFUL HINT:

Clutter can be controlled.

Have Some Fun

The idea is to dedicate our time to fun experiences rather than storing items. Imagine how much more you can enjoy life when you break the cycle of excess consumption.

Whether you are single, married, have children or don't have children, tailoring your house to suit your personal preferences is crucial. You want to make your home a special place that identifies with your lifestyle. Do everything you can to keep your home organized, peaceful, and clean. You'll feel glad you did each time you enter your space.

"Whatever we believe about ourselves and our ability comes true for us."

–Susan L. Taylor

CHAPTER 8

Check Those Spending Habits

Let me begin by saying that I am not in banking nor a finance guru, but it does not take a rocket scientist to know that sometimes we spend too much on unnecessary THINGS. Self-care is watching how you spend your money. Self-care with money is about guiding your cash flow with purpose. I'm not talking about going all-out chasing every dollar or transforming into a business mogul overnight. If that's what you want, then cool! It's more about being intentional with your funds. Right now I am definitely preaching to the choir, but since you're reading it When you get some cash, what's your game plan? What are your goals and intentions? Jot them down.

Let's get specific. Maybe you're trying to buy a new house – are you saving up for that down payment? Or perhaps you're dreaming of an extravagant trip – are you putting some funds away for that moment? Saving for your kids or grandkid's college fund, thinking about an investment property with buddies, buying new furniture, paying off your credit card or college debt, or even starting a new business – what's your money goal? We know that you need money for that goal and potential pitfalls.

That's the essence of self-care. It's about aligning your money with your dreams and desires. So, what's your next big money goal? That's your self-care outline right there. Trust me, without a plan, you're basically meandering through life without a compass. And let's be real, to truly shine, you've got to have some sort of plan.

Now, for some fun, let's toss in some lies. Maybe your 30-day goal involves funding a pet unicorn farm – totally valid. In 90 days, you could be investing in a spaceship for your intergalactic travels. Twelve months down the line, you might be the proud owner of a tropical island made entirely of milk chocolate. And five years from now, who knows, maybe you've set your sights on building a theme park dedicated to Hip-Hop and Country Music.

All jokes aside, having these goals outlined injects your finances with a sense of purpose. It's not just about the money; it's about chasing the lifestyle you're daydreaming about from time to time. So, spit it out right here, What's your money goal? It might be the self-care plan you didn't know you needed.

Financial specialist Arthur Anderson, CPFA®, founder of the Anderson ACE System®, emphasizes the importance of budgeting for financial stability. He suggests that everyone should have a budget to track their income and expenses, with the first priority being paying oneself. Anderson recommends allocating funds towards building an emergency fund and establishing an investment account, or alternatively, joining an investment club. These steps lay the foundation for a secure financial future.

"The more time you spend contemplating what you should have done...you lose valuable time planning what you can and will do."

– Lil Wayne

So, here's my plea: set yourself a money goal. Break it down the best you can and make it tangible. What's your money goal for the next 30 days?

What's your money game plan for the next 90 days? Plot it out. Just write your draft.

Hey, what about a year? Where do you see those funds taking you a year from now?

Lastly, let's dream big – what's your money master plan for the next five years?

Preventing Clutter at the Source

Preventing clutter right from the source is all about being proactive and adopting smart strategies to keep things in check. I've discussed some so if I have repeated myself, just take it as a reminder. Here are some tips that I find most effective in stopping clutter before it even begins:

-Thoughtful Shopping: Before buying something new, I always pause and ask myself if it's genuinely necessary and where it's going to live in my space. Avoiding impulse buys is super important.

-One In, One Out Rule: I've made it a habit to let go of something whenever I bring in a new item. If you bought a new shirt, it doesn't mean that you have to release or get rid of a shirt, it simply means that you have to part with something. It could be a pair of pants, a sweater, a tank top, dress or even a screwdriver if you're reaching really hard. The point is to part with something. It keeps the balance and prevents things from piling up unnecessarily. See *Additional Resources* for more about this rule.

-Declutter regularly. Set aside time to assess and declutter. It's a proactive approach that stops the chaos from building up.

-Embrace digital life. I'm talking about the benefits of going digital. Going paperless has been a lifesaver. Digital billing and filing systems significantly reduce paper clutter, and it's eco-friendly as well.

-Be intentional with your storage solutions. Investing in practical storage options is essential for maintaining an organized space. Not only does it keep things in order, but it also aids in the process of finding what you need when you need it.

-Start doing quick cleaning routines. The calendar is key! Little daily cleaning habits, like clearing countertops and putting things away, are a part of my routine. They help to maintain a space effortlessly.

-Organizational systems are important. Categorizing items and utilizing labels for containers, when necessary, can significantly contribute to a more streamlined and organized environment."

-Be mindful of sentimental items. While treasuring meaningful belongings is important, I've learned to set limits. Being selective about what sentimental items to keep prevents an overflow of emotional clutter.

-Family participation or support from friends and loved ones can be incredibly beneficial in the organization process. While it's ideal to have everyone on board, it's not always possible to receive the support we desire. However, don't let that be a barrier to your efforts. If you do have support from loved ones, educating them about the reasoning behind the placement of items in certain areas is key to ensuring everyone understands and respects the organizational system. This alignment ensures that everyone is on the same page, ultimately enhancing the organization process.

HELPFUL HINT:

It's about being proactive and making these strategies a natural part of your routine.

Strategies for Thoughtful Shopping

Buy what you need. Make a list. Think about what you need. Ask questions before you complete your purchase(s).

- How will you use the product you're considering?
- Do you already have enough similar items at home?
- Is this a necessity?

Focus on quality. In the long run, higher priced goods usually offer greater value. A fine cashmere sweater or sturdy kitchen knives may hold up for decades while bargain brands may need to be replaced annually. Ask yourself:

- Why in the world am I actually buying this thing?

- Is it really going to level up my lifestyle?

- Am I realistically going to get a lot of use out of it?

Stick to a budget. Decide in advance how much you can afford to spend. Regard occasional indulgences as an exception rather than the beginning of a habit.

Carry a list. Write down what you need to pick up before you leave home. Go straight to the stores and aisles where you can find your products.

Look away. The more time you spend wandering around sales displays and scrolling online because an ad popped up, the more likely you are to wind up with goods that sound like a bargain, but wind up as clutter. Don't be afraid to look away.

- Be especially careful at the checkout area that's designed to trigger impulse purchases.

- The goal is to not have to store items that we don't necessarily need.

Find other outlets. Retail therapy may be masking other issues.

- Find a hobby or do volunteer work if you're bored.

- Talk with a friend if you're feeling anxious or lonely.

- Get a therapist.

Buy for others. Studies show that spending money on others makes us happier than purchasing things for ourselves. Just a pro tip: make sure those gifts actually reach their destination. Opt for shipping – yeah, it might cost a little extra, but let's be real, is it really "more" when you've successfully completed your gifting mission? Nope, mission accomplished!

Strategies for Shopping Online

Alright, let's talk about online shopping. Don't let it pull you into its vortex. I mean, we both know not everything in that virtual cart is a must-have. Take a step back, revisit that list of questions, and hit yourself with some reality checks if necessary:

- First, how in the world are you planning to use this thing you're eyeing?

- Do you really need it, or do you currently have a bunch of similar stuff gathering dust?

- Is this purchase crossing over into the necessity boundary? Is it necessary?

- Why on earth am I really splurging on this item?

- Will it genuinely enhance my lifestyle?

- The crucial question here is, realistically, how much am I going to get out of it?

Giving yourself the third degree on these questions is like a sanity check for some shopping that might just turn into an unexpected adventure. I remember one day strolling down Michigan Avenue, I did way too much. Now, whenever I catch sight of one of those bags, I'm left shaking my head. There's this lingering feeling that I have to hang onto it because it cost a small fortune, but truth be told, it's not exactly my style. Selling them seems embarrassing, and I'm stuck in this dilemma. The moral of the story: make sure those buys sync up with your life and aren't just driven by impulsive urges.

Asking these questions might just save you from the impulse-buys. Keep that shopping in check.

- **Cool off.** Online purchases can pile up before you know it because there's no downtime for parking and commuting. *Try leaving items in* *your cart for at least 24 hours before making a final decision.* You may find you no longer want them once you have a chance to think further.

- **Pay off credit cards monthly.** Buying online is so easy it may not feel like real money. Avoiding credit card debt helps you monitor your spending and stabilize your finances.

- **Go to bed.** *The internet has no closing time so as an adult, you'll have to set your own curfew.* You'll feel fresher and richer in the morning if you turn off the computer and go to sleep.

Strategies for Shopping at Stores

Resist sales pressure. Be skeptical of limited time offers and long-term commitments. Tell sales clerks you need time to think, and do your own comparison shopping. Don't let freebies make you feel obligated to buy something in return.

Next time you're at the mall or buying online, remember that today's clutter is yesterday's shopping spree. Save time and money by accumulating less. You and your home will come out ahead.

How to Make Your To-Do List More Effective

You already know that to-do lists help you get focused and organized throughout the day. *When you have your to-do list in hand, you're freeing your mind from all the disorganized thoughts and, instead, getting them down on paper.*

However, this technique can go awry if your to-do list isn't organized as well as it should be. You might lose your motivation and drive and, at the end of the day, you may notice that most of the things from your list are not crossed off.

1. **Clarify Priorities.** It may help you to develop some sort of ranking system for your to-do list. Certainly every item on the list can't be equally important. You can even use a number system and rank them

from 1 to 5. Items ranked 1 might have a lower priority, while the 5s are tasks you should attend to first.

- You should also clarify your priorities in the sense that you need to leave yourself detailed instructions. Figure out the: who, what, where, when and why of items that may be complicated. This way, when it comes time to tackle the task, you won't skip over them simply because they seem too complex to complete.

2. **Pare Down the List.** You need to complete tasks or part of tasks one step at a time. If you have 15 minutes to spare, find something on the list that you can complete in that time period. It's common to tell yourself that 15 minutes is not enough time to do something, but all those 15-minute chunks add up to something huge. At the end of the day you'll be surprised how much you've accomplished in small increments.

3. **Include Flex Time.** If your to-do list is too rigid, it simply won't be effective. You absolutely need to include some flexibility and breathing room in your day. Try not to jam pack your day with unreasonable goals, otherwise, you'll be at risk of disappointment.

4. **Add in Something Fun.** Your to-do list is no doubt full of things you may not be looking forward to doing. That's why integrating fun activities and tasks should also be a priority! When you add in a fun item it doesn't feel like work. It may even feel like a break. When you return to the less desirable items, you'll be more motivated to actually get them done.

5. **Don't List Too Much.** *It's vital not to overwhelm yourself.* While some days might be action packed in order to reach certain deadlines, you need to avoid this level of stress on a regular basis. If there's too much on your plate, or you have to work too fast, you can't possibly enjoy yourself and you'll only end up frustrated and overwhelmed.

"Not everything that is faced can be changed, but nothing can be changed until it is faced."

—James Baldwin

CHAPTER 9

Digital Life

We live in a world of technology. There's so much technology that sometimes we have to unplug to reset and get back to the basics. Face it, we have to use technology to our advantage. With using it over the years there has been an accumulation of digital junk that we house without even knowing sometimes. Junk is junk rather if it's on your phone, in your house, on a tablet or a computer and it has to be handled.

Digital Clutter

People have thousands of photos jamming their smartphones. They also have an excessive number of files cluttering their computers. Have you ever made a PowerPoint presentation? Let's not even talk about the screenshots. I tell myself that they are notes for things that I aspire to do. I have SO MANY

NOTES! What about the old cords, the chargers, and earphones that are tangled up into other stuff?

We now have digital clutter that needs to be simplified or released because we don't know what it is or its origin. That junk drawer is full of this type of stuff (e.g. random batteries, electrical tape, more head phones, mini tablets). Simplifying how you handle your digital life is important.

Begin Decluttering Your Digital Life

Prioritize emails, newsletters and so on. Only keep the things that really matter. Is anything cluttering up your computer's hard drive? Go through your email(s) inbox and delete those you don't need or file them.

Checking emails is an integral part of my end-of-week digital declutter routine. During this time, I dedicate myself to responding to any outstanding emails and organizing older emails into their respective folders. By doing this, I ensure that my inbox remains streamlined and focused solely on the projects I'm actively engaged in. This approach helps me maintain clarity and efficiency in managing my emails, allowing me to stay on top of my tasks and commitments.

Clean up your computer desktop and delete old files or back them up to an external drive. Take the time to properly back up your files, so you never lose important work. Clearing out old files is like straightening up a cluttered room—it just feels good. Every now and then, I make it a point to go through my digital stash and weed out anything I don't need anymore.

I start by sorting through my files and folders, looking for stuff that's outdated or just taking up space. If I haven't touched it in months and it's not something I know I'll need in the future, it's outta there. But of course, I'm careful about it. I double-check to make sure I'm not tossing anything important or sensitive. And when I'm really sure, I hit that delete button.

By doing this regularly, I keep my digital space neat and organized, making it easier to find what I need when I need it. Plus, it's like a weight off my shoulders knowing I'm not hoarding unnecessary files. So, if you're feeling bogged down by digital clutter, give it a try. Trust me, it's worth it.

Paperless Option

In the midst of our hectic schedules, managing appointments can be a real challenge. The good news is, there's a plethora of tools out there catering to different preferences and lifestyles.

Going paperless in this digital age is popular. It cuts out the paper to save yourself some organizational headaches and helps the environment. When companies bill you, there is usually an option to go paperless. If you aren't already, use this option and start managing your billing statements online. Remember that you'll have less physical paper to file and/or shred.

Smartphone Clutter

I really dislike upgrading my cell phones due to the long wait of backloading all of my information. So now what I do is take advantage of those waiting times like waiting in the doctor's office, dentist office, waiting for the hair stylist or when getting a pedicure. You get the point. When waiting I delete apps that I haven't used in a long time which are using a lot of my data.

Believe me, you don't want to be somewhere special and your phone won't allow you to take another picture.

Do yourself a favor.....

1. Get rid of apps you don't use anymore. They're just taking up space.

2. Hide those apps you only open once in a blue moon. No need for them to clutter up your screen.

3. Make folders to group similar apps together. It's similar to organizing your desk drawers.

4. Consider sorting your apps by topic which makes finding them easier.

5. Customize your app organization however you like. Use emojis, arrange by usage—you do you.

6. Save space by storing stuff like photos and documents in the cloud.

7. Don't let old messages pile up. Archive or delete them regularly.

8. Take control of your notifications. Cut down on the clutter and only keep the ones you really need.

Business Contacts

Make your business contacts digital. Start a list of all your business contacts somewhere on your computer, such as your address book in your email. Keep track of their business name, photos, phone number, mailing address, and email addresses. This way you can toss out those old business cards that may be piling up on your desk. Chances are that you will be throwing away lots because you either have them in your contacts already or don't remember who they are in the first place.

Appointments

In our fast-paced lives, staying on top of appointments can be quite a juggling act. Thankfully, there are plenty of tools out there designed to make this task a whole lot easier. From digital calendars to smart scheduling apps, there's a tool for every preference and lifestyle. So, whether you're a tech-savvy guru or prefer the classic pen-and-paper method, finding the right tool can be a game-changer in keeping your schedule on point.

Marcell Wade, an educator and socialite, shared: "Utilizing my calendar is an essential aspect of managing my schedule effectively. It's crucial for me to input all of my appointments, family gatherings, doctor visits, and other reminders to ensure that I don't miss any commitments. My friends and I maintain a shared calendar for upcoming events and birthdays, facilitating seamless coordination. Unfortunately, I recently overlooked an event because it wasn't added to my calendar, resulting in a missed opportunity."

Marcell's recommendation to utilize tools like Apple or Google Calendar for scheduling is invaluable for avoiding oversights and ensuring efficient planning. When I receive an invite via text for a party or gathering, I instinctively turn to Google Calendar to create an appointment. This proactive approach not only helps me organize my schedule, but also allows him to invite others who he is considering taking with him.

By leveraging digital calendars, such as Apple or Google Calendar, people can integrate event details into their schedules, set reminders, and share invitations with friends or colleagues. This process minimizes the risk of forgetting important engagements and facilitates coordination with others.

In today's fast-paced world, where schedules can quickly fill up with various commitments, relying on digital calendar tools is a practical solution for staying organized and maximizing productivity. Marcell's approach exemplifies the effectiveness of incorporating technology into everyday life to enhance efficiency and ensure nothing falls through the cracks.

Face it, people live really busy lifestyles. There are many tools that you can use to stay on point with appointments. Use one that resonates with you. More are listed in the Additional Resources section of this book.

"*If you prioritize yourself, you are going to save yourself.*"

—**Gabrielle Union**

Conclusion

Becoming organized is a game-changer. It's like flipping a switch from chaos to clarity, from stress to serenity. When everything has its place, you can focus and get things done without that constant worry gnawing at you.

And it's not just about feeling good—it's about building trust. Whether it's in business or personal relationships, being organized shows reliability. People know they can count on you, and that's invaluable.

Sometimes the thought of getting organized can feel overwhelming, especially when life pulls you in a million directions. That's when a helping hand can make all the difference. It doesn't have to be someone with all the answers, just someone who's there for you, cheering you on as you tackle the chaos.

If you need a little extra push, that's where I come in. As a daughter, educator, business owner, and organization enthusiast, I've seen it all. Together, we'll slay the clutter and create a space where you can thrive.

I want you to remember that Rome wasn't built in a day. Small steps lead to big changes. Start with one corner, one drawer, one routine at a time. Before you know it, you'll have systems in place that keep things running smoothly. The benefits? Your progress might just exceed your expectations. When your life is organized, you see things more clearly. Solutions come easier, and you have more time for the things that bring you joy.

So here's to taking action, one step at a time. You've got this! Please do yourself a favor: Organize, Simplify and Thrive. Clear your way to the lifestyle that will allow you to thrive.

"You don't make progress by standing on the sidelines, whimpering and complaining. You make progress by implementing ideas."

—Shirley Chisholm

Additional Resources

"One In, One Out Rule"

This rule is a great practice for maintaining a clutter-free and manageable living space. By adopting this rule, you not only prevent unnecessary accumulation of items, but also encourage a more mindful approach to consumption. Here are some benefits and tips for implementing the "One In, One Out" rule effectively:

Benefits:

- Encourages mindfulness: By consciously evaluating what items you bring into your space, you become more aware of your consumption habits.

- Promotes decluttering: Requiring you to part with something whenever you acquire a new item helps prevent clutter from building up over time.

- Saves space: Keeping a balance between incoming and outgoing items ensures that your living space remains organized and spacious.

- Saves money: By being selective about what you bring in, you're less likely to make impulse purchases and can save money in the long run.

Tips for implementing the rule:

- Set clear guidelines: Define what constitutes an "item" to prevent loopholes. For example, if you buy a set of kitchen utensils, consider whether each utensil counts individually or as a set.

- Regular assessments: Periodically review your possessions to identify items that no longer serve you or have been replaced by newer acquisitions.

- Donate or recycle: Instead of simply discarding items, consider donating them to charity or recycling them whenever possible.

- Focus on quality over quantity: Prioritize acquiring high-quality items that you truly need and love, rather than accumulating a large quantity of possessions.

- Be flexible: While the rule encourages mindful consumption, allow yourself some flexibility to adapt it to your needs and circumstances.

The "One In, One Out" rule promotes an intentional and organized lifestyle.

Makeup: How Long Do I Keep It?

PAO stands for Period After Opening, and it's a nifty little symbol you'll often find on product packaging. What's so neat about the PAO is that it gives you the lowdown on how long a product will last after you pop it open for the first time. It's like having a built-in expiration date specifically tailored to when you start using the product. So, the next time you spot that little PAO symbol, you'll know exactly how long you've got before it's time to bid farewell to your favorite skincare or beauty product.

Mascaras and eyeliners— 3-6 months

While some brands might clue you in with a PAO symbol or an expiration date, if you're not seeing any guidance, here's the deal: aim to toss them out within three to six months after cracking them open.

Now, there's been some back and forth about mascara being a bacteria hotspot, but some studies have shared that its low moisture content means it's not as much of a breeding ground as we once thought. Still, your mascara wand and product can collect dirt and oils, which isn't ideal given they're getting close to your precious peepers.

Foundation and concealer— Up to 1 year

These products typically last around a year. But here's the kicker: when your compact foundation starts cracking or your liquid products start separating or congealing, it's time today goodbye. Oh, and if anything starts smelling weird to you, it's time to pass it on—time to toss it out, no ifs, ands, or buts.

Powder Products (Eyeshadow, Blush, Setting Powder)— Up to 2 years

If properly sanitized, powder products can last up to two years. Spritzing them with alcohol is a good practice to help kill bacteria and prolong their life.

To maintain the integrity of powder products, it's important to keep them dry and avoid introducing moisture into the containers.

Lip Products

- Lipsticks
- Chapsticks
- Lip Glosses
- Liquid Lipsticks

—Lipsticks and chapsticks should typically be replaced after about a year due to the risk of bacterial buildup, especially in products that come into direct contact with the lips.

—Liquid lipsticks and lip glosses, especially those in tubes, can harbor bacteria more easily due to their liquid consistency and applicator design.

—Sanitizing lipstick can sometimes help extend its lifespan, but it's important to monitor the product for any changes in texture, smell, or color, which could indicate that it's gone bad.

Where to Keep Makeup

Store makeup products in a cool, dry place away from direct sunlight to help preserve their quality and prevent bacterial growth.

> **HELPFUL TIP:**
>
> Pay attention to expiration dates and signs of spoilage, such as changes in smell, texture, or color, and discard products accordingly.

EARN MONEY: ONLINE PLATFORMS

There are several online platforms such as ThredUp where you can declutter your closet and earn money by selling your gently used clothing, shoes, and accessories. Here are a few alternatives:

- Poshmark is a social commerce marketplace where you can sell new or gently used fashion items directly to other users. You can list your items for sale, set your own prices, and handle the shipping process.

- Depop is a peer-to-peer shopping app where you can buy and sell unique fashion items. It's popular among fashion enthusiasts, vintage collectors, and independent sellers. You can list your items for sale, interact with buyers, and manage your sales directly through the app.

- Mercari is an online marketplace where you can sell a variety of items, including clothing, accessories, electronics, and more. You can list your items for sale, set your own prices, and ship them directly to buyers using Mercari's prepaid shipping labels.

- eBay is one of the largest online marketplaces where you can sell a wide range of items, including clothing and accessories. You can list your items for auction or set a fixed price, and manage your sales through eBay's platform.

- Facebook Marketplace allows you to buy and sell items locally within your community. You can list your clothing, shoes, and accessories for sale, set your own prices, and arrange for pickup or shipping with buyers.

- Tradesy specializes in selling pre-owned designer fashion items, including clothing, handbags, shoes, and accessories. You can list your items for sale, set your own prices, and Tradesy handles the shipping process.

HELPFUL TIP/PLEASE READ:

"Please note that while these online platforms offer convenient ways to declutter your closet and potentially earn money by selling your items, it's essential to use them at your own discretion. Each platform has its own policies, terms of service, and community guidelines that users are expected to follow. Additionally, personal information such as usernames, addresses, and payment details may be required when using these platforms, so it's important to exercise caution and protect your privacy. Be mindful of scams, fraudulent buyers or sellers, and always conduct transactions in a safe and secure manner. Ultimately, the decision to use these sites rests with you, and it's important to weigh the benefits and risks before participating in online selling activities."

How Long Does Nail Polish Last?

Myra Dunbar, a respected nail care specialist, emphasizes the importance of proper nail polish storage and maintenance to ensure optimal performance and longevity. Here's a breakdown of her insights:

Shelf Life of Nail Polish:

- Myra suggests that nail polishes typically have a shelf life of up to two years, while gel polish can last up to three years when stored correctly.

- Understanding the shelf life of your nail polish helps you gauge its freshness and effectiveness.

Storage Recommendations:

- Myra recommends storing unopened polish bottles in cool, dark places to extend their lifespan and maintain their smooth texture.

- Proper storage conditions can prevent premature drying, thickening, or color changes in the polish.

Avoid Unnecessary Accumulation:

- Myra advises against holding onto nail polish unnecessarily, implying that decluttering your collection can lead to better results when applying polish.

- Regularly assessing and decluttering your nail polish collection helps prevent the accumulation of expired or unusable products.

Signs of Deterioration:

- Myra highlights the importance of monitoring nail polish for signs of deterioration, such as discoloration, texture changes, or consistency issues.

- These indicators may suggest the presence of unhealthy bacteria or chemical buildup in the polish, which can compromise its quality and performance.

By following Myra Dunbar's recommendations for nail polish care and storage, you can prolong the lifespan of your personal products and ensure a consistently high-quality nail care experience. Regularly assessing your nail polish collection for signs of deterioration and decluttering when necessary helps maintain a healthy and vibrant nail care routine.

"If you are free, you need to free somebody else. If you have some power, then your job is to empower somebody else.

–Toni Morrison

Testimonials

"Love To Organize You Changed My Life!

First, just let me say that Sylvia is the sweetest and she's extremely professional! Secondly, she changed my life! I absolutely HATE organizing and everything that comes with it. I have anxiety when trying to organize and Sylvia's smile warmed my home (and my closets)!

I had a coat closet, pantry, and three clothing closets for Sylvia to help me organize. She held me (and my husband) accountable on items we needed to purge and helped with organizing our clothes. Her attention to detail is immaculate. Her patience is unmatched! She happily dealt with me and my anxiety and I'm sure no task is too small for her!

I love Sylvia and her services and have recommended her to my friends and family! I have more tasks I plan to have her help me with. She is truly the best in the game!"

Chicari Cole

"As a mental health provider who has experienced the benefits of an organized closet with the support of Sylvia, I can attest to its ability to reduce stress and enhance clarity. I call her The Closet Whisperer for a reason."

Dr. Nyela Malone

"Her expert advice on how to declutter while unlocking your potential is a tour of self-discovery. She teaches you how to clear out the clutter and create space for clarity, focus, and new endeavors."

Nicole Fike

"As a busy mom of two and dedicated educator, the tools and resources in this book have helped organize my life tremendously. The clear and detailed advice was easy to follow and became a part of my daily routine."

Alexandra Dennis

"Working alongside Sylvia as she orchestrated a wedding was an absolute pleasure. Her meticulous planning and attention to detail were evident throughout the process. As an artist, I was contracted to provide support, and it was inspiring to witness Sylvia's vision come to life. Needless to say, the wedding was nothing short of amazing."

BRYANTlamont

"Relax and take notes..."

—The Notorious B.I.G.

Made in the USA
Monee, IL
02 June 2024